AESTHETICS:
AN INTRODUCTION

Ruth L. Saw, formerly Professor of Philosophy
at Birkbeck College, is Professor Emeritus of Aesthetics at the University of London. She was a
founding member and is currently President of the
British Society of Aesthetics and was Vice-President
of the Aristotelian Society. She is the author of
The Vindication of Metaphysics and *Leibniz.*

AESTHETICS:
An Introduction

By RUTH L. SAW

ANCHOR BOOKS

DOUBLEDAY & COMPANY, INC.

GARDEN CITY, NEW YORK

1971

Anchor Books edition: 1971
Library of Congress Catalog Card Number 71–144309
Copyright © 1971 by Ruth L. Saw
All Rights Reserved
Printed in the United States of America
First Edition

Preface

It is impossible for a professor emeritus to acknowl-edge adequately the contribution made to his opin-ions and ideas by the many people with whom he has been in contact—his colleagues, his students, his friends. All that he can do is to thank them in a general way for the many discussions in class, both seminars and tutorials, and hope that they will be pleased if they recognize our former exchanges. However, I can thank specifically one of my former students, Professor D. J. O'Connor, the editor of this series, who has carefully read and commented on this book. He made many valuable suggestions, most of which I acted upon. I also wish to thank Mrs. Susan Cunnew for compiling the bibliography, and my friends Mrs. Joan Edwards and Miss Grace Lyford for their help in proofreading, checking ref-erences, and many other similar tasks.

ACKNOWLEDGMENTS

I acknowledge, with thanks, permission from the Editors of *Philosophy*, *The Proceedings of the Aristotelian Society*, and *The British Journal of Aesthetics* to reprint articles, as follows:

Chapter I. *The British Journal of Aesthetics*, October, 1969.
Chapter II. *Philosophy*, January, 1961.
Chapter VI (in part). *Proceedings of the Aristotelian Society*, Supplementary Volume, 1962.

R. L. S.

Contents

AESTHETICS:
AN INTRODUCTION

CHAPTER I

The Tasks of Aesthetics

In the course of my teaching life I have approached
the problems of aesthetics in varying ways according to the changing fashions of discussion. I have,
however, found no reason to change my opinion as
to what were the problems and their importance,
though they may be thought of now as outmoded.
There are fashions in ways of thinking as there are
in dress; and just as one may hang on to a favorite
frock knowing that in time it will become fashionable again, so one may preserve one's way of thinking knowing that it will reappear later as "the
thing." Nevertheless I feel it incumbent on me to
present some kind of justification, even an "apology," for calling on my readers to consider with me
such problems as the logic of the judgment of taste,
its objectivity, and other such topics that aestheticians today seem to find wearisome in the extreme.
I am hoping to engage your interest and cooperation in my enterprise, which I think a worthy one,
not in the sense that I have worthily carried it out,
but in the sense that it was worth a serious attempt.
I accept as just the criticism made at the meeting

of the British Society of Aesthetics to which I presented this chapter, that my "apology" was not for aesthetics generally, but only for my own brand. However, I add that one naturally thinks that what one is doing is the suitable thing to do. It will appear in the sequel how much I appreciate the work of aestheticians who would not appreciate mine! I must add, further, that my appreciation of their work is of what I take to be an interesting and valuable but peripheral contribution to what is my main concern.

In spite of the criticism noted above, I pose as my opening question, "Why aesthetics?" This might be a particular case of the general question, "Why philosophy?" and the people who raise it would apply it also to logic, ethics, metaphysics, and to all the other branches of philosophy. We recall Locke's remark, "God has not been so sparing to men to make them barely two-legged creatures and left it to Aristotle to make them rational."[1] People in general dislike discussion and are always seeking ways to bring it to a close. They differ merely in the point at which their tolerance disappears. Some men will not go one step beyond the factual question, and if one can by any means bring them to reflect upon a philosophical problem, their reflection will produce no more than the practical question, "Does it matter?"

Among the branches of philosophy, however, the question may be posed peculiarly in relation to aesthetics. It differs, for example, from logic in that

[1] *Essay Concerning Human Understanding*, IV. xvii. 4.

there is nothing in it comparable to our confident calling on men to agree that if all men are mortal and Socrates is a man, then Socrates is mortal. (I leave out of account modern problems about the syllogism. Any such account would go far beyond anything that a plain man ought to be called on to consider.) Again, while it is true that some might consider moral judgment to be, like the aesthetic, a matter of opinion, nevertheless we have the ethos of Judaism, of Christianity, of Hinduism, and so on, to which there is nothing whatever comparable in our aesthetic evaluations. Still more does aesthetics entirely lack any such sanction as the legal systems of the world have, with their attempts, however imperfect, to embody abstract justice. Metaphysics is lent respectability by its connection with mathematics and physics, and epistemology by its connection with psychology and physiology. Aesthetics alone has no recourse to any established system of evaluations or of knowledge. Therefore it has its own version of the point of "disappearance of tolerance." This may occur at any one of three stages. First, some artists enjoy technical discussion with their fellows and no other kind of discussion whatever. Some artists, of course do not wish to engage in even this kind of discussion, but we do not need to consider the point at which their tolerance disappears; it never even made an appearance! Second, some appreciators enjoy technical criticism, but dismiss any other kind of critical discourse. Many of these are amateur practitioners. Third, there are appreciators who enjoy talk about pictures, plays, music, etc., carried one stage further, to include, perhaps, the intentions of the artist, (a) in a technical sense—"The two hands touching carry the eye across the canvas," or (b) in a "meaningful" sense—"The two hands touching present a symbol of . . ." Some would tolerate (a) but not (b). After this point we may be led away into program notes, catalogues of art exhibitions, even blurbs on the covers of books, and here anyone may be excused for opting out.

The stage beyond is intolerable to everyone except philosophers. It is especially repugnant to practitioners of the arts and even (or I might here even add "especially") it is repugnant to those whom one might expect to be sympathetic—the professional appreciators of the arts, notably art historians, who, however they may end up, started out as ardent appreciators of the arts. This gives us our first problem, that the people most concerned with the arts are most antagonistic to the concern of philosophers with the arts. I except those concerned with the literary arts, who are in the special position of using words to investigate and evaluate the arts that have words as their instruments, so that they are more likely to be tolerant of the aesthetician's use of words if he writes well, and even to be led on to consider what he is saying. Students coming from art history to the study of aesthetics are apt to come forewarned by their professors of the irrelevance of much of what they are now to be called upon to consider. Their professors have carefully and habitually claimed a disinterest in, and even an incapacity for, evaluation. "I can teach you to recognize examples of styles, genres, etc., but not to pronounce them good," they say. "If I use the word 'good,' it merely means a good example of Baroque architecture, or . . ." If one raises the question why one should bother to study these particular examples, or these examples of that particular style, one is merely being vexatious unless the question means that one is interested in the place of this piece of work or this style in the general history of art.

Our next problem concerns philosophers who disclaim an interest in the specific problems of aesthetics, but who nevertheless feel a proprietary interest in some other branch of philosophy and so feel entitled to criticize what they claim to be "silly" theories, such as the theory that music may be called "sad," or still worse that one may think of the composer as "expressing sadness." They come out from a discussion saying things like, "What nonsense! Everyone knows that X was having the time of his life in Paris when he was supposed to be expressing melancholy in his compositions, and will you please tell me how he managed to preserve his melancholy over the months in which he was composing?" They do not realize that these objections have been raised and met many times, and I have no doubt that they will go on being raised while there are people who think they know it all without bothering to find out.

At least these philosophers disclaim an interest in aesthetics; there is an even more regrettable group of philosophers who call themselves aestheticians, but who have in fact abdicated, we might even say that they have "sold the pass." They go through the list of topics: Intentions of the artist? If relevant, a matter for psychologists. The usefulness of art? If social, this is for sociologists; if individual, for psychologists. One aesthetician of my acquaintance came to London all the way from Uppsala, Sweden, to attend a conference on the teaching of aesthetics, to express the opinion that aesthetics, like psychology at the beginning of the century, was ready to drop off the tree of philosophy. His discussions of the writers of aesthetics proper seemed to show that he considered his function to be the pointing out of their lack of psychological and sociological concern; but his concern with such writings seemed to me to show an uneasy sense that after all they were saying something important that was not allowed for in his philosophy.

The cause of these dissatisfactions may be stated quite briefly: it is that aesthetics is unique among the evaluative disciplines in that it has to do, importantly, with feelings, feelings expressed in art and in the appreciation of art, and with the judgments that are usually taken to be based on these feelings. It is then easily assumed that since feelings are sheer matters of fact about which it would be nonsensical to say that we ought or ought not to have them, they are to be suitably treated only by a science of some sort. I take Kant's most important contribution to be the demonstration of the proper way to deal with feeling in aesthetics.[2] This must be dealt with more fully, but here we may simply

[2] *Critique of Judgment*, trans. J. H. Bernard, London, 1914. P. 47.

point out that feelings enter also into mathematics and logic. People are willing to say that a judgment of approval is merely an expression of feeling in the evaluation of art, or even of conduct, but not in the evaluation of an argument or a calculation. This comparison is not as perverse as many people will find it, as I hope to show later. We may also point out that people are far too willing to acquiesce in the view that there is nothing to be done about feelings but to enjoy or suffer them. Here we may recall Aristotle's view that moral education consists in the attaching of feeling to its proper object.[3] There are many cases on record of this redirection of feeling. When Saul was converted on the road to Damascus, the zeal and ardor he had displayed in his persecution of the Christians were not removed but turned towards a different object. Similarly, in the appreciation of art we must admit that it is a sheer matter of fact that a certain feeling is aroused in us when we look at pictures or see a play, but we may regret that we do or do not enjoy this particular object. We may know that we are far too easily pleased by associations with childhood scenes and may know that we feel pleasure in a less worthy object, and we may know that, given time, we could become capable of enjoying difficult art and put ourselves to school until we either succeed or have to accept with regret a blind or deaf spot.

At this point it will probably be objected that even if I have made my point, and it is agreed that

---

[3] *Nicomachaean Ethics,* trans. Frank H. Peters, London, 1881. Bk. 2, Sect. 3.

this attaching of an emotion to an appropriate object is an important activity, it still remains to be
shown that it is not more efficiently and suitably
carried out by the critics. If this were so, I would
give up aesthetics; but I do not think it is so. When
Nathan said to David, "Thou art the man," he was
counting on David's seeing, once it was pointed
out to him, that the rich man's killing of the poor
man's one ewe lamb was comparable to his own
taking of the wife of Uriah the Hittite. This was
pointed out to him by his moral mentor, not by a
philosopher. But it is the moral philosopher who
reflects upon the importance of the similarity and
enunciates the principle that what mine is to me,
yours is to you. It may be said that this is so obvious
that it does not need pointing out; but unless there
is someone in the background continually saying
these things, it will not be long before they pass
out of the currency of human thinking. It is true
that in aesthetic education it is the critic who
points out the features of a work and leads the
spectator to say that he now sees the work properly
and will be able to enjoy it. But it is the aesthetician who reflects upon the transformation and can
say why it is that the spectator is now in a "better"
state than he was before. Imagine a young man
with a collection of beauties on the lids of chocolate boxes. (I leave it to my younger readers to
supply a more up-to-date example.) Many people
would be concerned for this young man even
though they might hold theories of taste that made
their concern unreasonable. It would be aestheticians who would be concerned to establish the na-

ture of the concern, and its rationality or otherwise.

We still have to come to the most damaging criticism of all, since it admits all that we have so far claimed and still thinks aesthetics outmoded. It may be expressed as follows: "Yes, there is a literature of aesthetics, a tradition of the treatment of its problems, and there are certainly questions which you may claim as yours; but they are a poor remnant after the socially important and useful ones have been allocated each to its appropriate discipline. You can continue to talk about the logic of the aesthetic judgment and its objectivity, but such talk has no utility. If you engage in it, it is for its own sake; but why you should want to, passes my comprehension. It is not as if it yielded a beautiful system as does symbolic logic. It is worth doing only for itself, and it is not worth doing for itself." I will now attempt a positive defense of aesthetics directed specifically against this last attack.

A short reply would be that I personally very much enjoy reflecting upon the similarities and differences between aesthetic judgments on the one hand and moral, logical, and scientific judgments on the other. I agree wholeheartedly with Leibniz, too, when he says that one must go to the limits of what can be done with argument. If we are led to the brink and draw back, we are abdicating our function as philosophers. It is not the concern of anyone but philosophers, who begin asking questions where everyone else stops, but it *is* our concern to analyze and set out the interrelationships of aesthetic judgments actually made by plain men and by critics and to examine the concepts used in critical and ordinary discourse. I think it even more important, though I expect little sympathy here, that we should do our best to establish the objectivity of the aesthetic judgment. Why, it is said, should we bother our heads about a judgment that as a matter of fact is rarely, if ever, made? How many times do we find anyone asserting categorically that *this* is absolutely beautiful? To quote the late Professor J. L. Austin: "Would you not be more profitably engaged in examining the 'dainty and the dumpy' rather than the 'beautiful and the ugly'?"[4] The answer is "Yes, certainly, in the ordinary way." We all know by now that absolutes do not exist, that all our measurements cluster around, say, the yard and never coincide with it exactly. All the more reason, then, for not abandoning our actual bronze bar which constitutes our standard, or what meaning could we give to "clustering around"? The whole system of assessments would become chaos if we did not keep in mind or in physical fact some standard in terms of which our assessments are more or less accurate.

Still, I wish to make a more positive—and more controversial—claim. It is that the study of aesthetics is of the utmost human utility. At this point I laid down my pen and asked myself seriously whether I was being perverse or would really stand by this opinion. I looked back over a long life spent

---

[4] "A Plea for Excuses," *Philosophical Papers*, p. 131. Originally published in *Proceedings of the Aristotelian Society*, Session 1956/57, New Series, Vol. 57.

in the teaching and study of philosophy, and I saw that for me metaphysics and aesthetics have constituted the disciplines most apt for the correction and development of complete persons. These two disciplines rely on the complementary notions of universality and individuality. The great metaphysicians of the seventeenth century, Spinoza and Leibniz, who were also mathematicians, were able, predictably from my point of view, to make a place for individuals in their vast schemes of the universe. At first sight this is a ridiculous claim. Are not mathematicians and metaphysicians of all people the most concerned with what is universal and necessary and not with what is particular and simply existent? Are not their vast spatiotemporal schemes inimical to the mere parts of matter that move uncertainly about within them? Not at all—each such part owes its very peculiarities to its position within the scheme, so that we have a "this" which is what it is in virtue of its place in the universe. Moreover, the universals of mathematics—triangles, circles, and so on—have the saving peculiarity of not having instances in the ordinary sense of the word. We may much more confidently speak of "the triangle" than of "the child." The "natural" scientists have to be contented to use that miserable notion, beloved of empiricists, of "what is for the most part," and we may think of their notions as figments of the mind, fabricated for the sake of formulating general truths and having no other status. It is far otherwise with the objects of mathematics.

A related concern of aesthetics is the wholeness and integrity of a work of art, an integrity that is closely patterned on that of the human person. Moreover the continual testing of principle by appeal to particular cases gives a suppleness to the mind and to the emotions, together with a bracing of thought by recourse back to the universal. Furthermore, the continual attempt to understand our enjoyments and distastes, and to correct those which seem to us unwarranted or disproportionate, plays a large part in increasing our self-knowledge.

I now come to my positive account of the social usefulness of the study of aesthetics, and I first call on you to notice the terrible vulnerability of the man in the street. He is usually taken as the example of pure common sense when what is meant is his credulity where a cynical attitude is concerned. It is fatally easy to induce him to take the first step into skepticism and leave him there. Any teacher of philosophy knows how easy it is to induce beginners to become skeptics, and it is salutary to startle the young in this way. It would be unforgivable, however, if one did not know that they were to be introduced to the history of such ideas and shown how they had been offered and rejected many times over. Those who have given up their time to a certain study have this study as their proper work, but they also have a duty to see that the uninformed are not exploited by half-truths. It is the easiest thing in the world to persuade people that there is no disputing about tastes without giving them any inkling that there is anything to be said on the other side, especially if they have a vague kind of feeling that it is "scientific" and "modern" to think in this way. Many people preface their remarks with "Science has shown that . . . ," and they vaguely feel that, given more time and training, they could produce a proof that entitles them to claim that their beliefs are rationally held. It may be objected that these considerations have no bearing on the deliberations of philosophers among themselves; but ideas debated at the academic level seep through to more everyday thinking in time, and an idea that is hedged about with all kinds of modifications in serious thinking becomes current with the saving clauses disregarded. (Of course, if it had ever been or could ever be conclusively shown that no man's taste is better than another's, what I have just said would not be relevant. I am not asking for the acceptance of "useful myth," but that useful possible truths should be seriously and sympathetically examined.)

A common statement of the plain man's position is "I know what I like." This is taken by himself to be a bold assertion of sturdy common sense, and by the aesthete to be an expression of Philistinism. But is it true? Does he as a matter of fact know what he likes, or is this not one of those oversimplifications induced by a no-standard position? Sir Joshua Reynolds urged his students to acquaint themselves with the history of their art and with its great manifestations. He related how he found himself in Rome not knowing how to look or what to look for, vaguely aware that something magnificent was there for him to see but feeling hopelessly miserable, bewildered, and confused.[5] How inadequate it would have been to ask him whether he "liked" those paintings. He probably would have answered, "I am going to!" We have only to watch a child trying to find out whether he likes a new flavor to see how false it is to suppose that this is a question that always has a simple answer. His face takes on a succession of expressions while he wonders whether to give way to enjoyment or distaste. It probably will be objected here that if it were simply a question of the flavor, the child would be able to give a direct answer, but that it is complicated by people standing by, anxious for him to say that he likes it. This is theory. But even if it were so, are not our aesthetic judgments complicated in just this way? Someone thinks we ought or ought not to like this thing. It might again be objected that even with complex states of mind we surely ought to be able to say whether they are pleasant or not. I think this is debatable. But even if it were established, it would not follow that because we found ourselves in a pleasant state in the presence of a given object, we should be able to say that we liked that object. It may be true that in very mild cases of pleasure or pain we recognize these qualities, but let a little excitement enter in and our certainty about our state goes. We have only to reflect on the havoc wrought in our estimations of the

[5] *Memoirs of Sir Joshua Reynolds*, ed. Henry Beechy, London, 1852. Vol. I, p. 61. Throughout his discourses, Reynolds repeatedly urges his students to acquaint themselves with the history of their art; but his description of his bewilderment appears in the *Memoirs*.

worth of objects by nostalgia to see how risky it is to assert that we know what we like. (Contrary to the usual notion, nostalgia is not an affliction of the old alone. Mary Hopkin was top of the pops for six weeks running, singing in a sad little-girl's voice, "Those were the days!")

Aestheticians, then, have it as their duty to supply the stiffening to what would otherwise be an amorphous mass of expressions of feeling, opinion, and theory. They should not emulate some modern teachers of literature who think that children should be allowed to enjoy poetry without worrying about grammar. Some children positively like grammar. But quite apart from this, some teachers tend to forget their own enjoyment of literature might owe quite a lot to a feeling for its "bony structure" fostered by their own salutary drilling in grammar in the past.

My discussion so far may be summed up as an attempt to present aesthetics as a branch of philosophy. It will become increasingly difficult to maintain this viewpoint, even if to do so were wholly desirable, but the least and the most one can do at this stage is to give some idea of one's own peculiarities of aesthetic preference. My own have become clear to me in the course of my aesthetic studies. First, then, natural beauty moves me more strongly than the beauty of art, and since this is so I enjoy two very different types of aesthetic experience. In art, the enjoyment of objects in isolation is possible and indeed necessary. In nature, the rhythm of the seasons, the different flavor of landscape at dawn, at high noon, and at sunset, under rain, clouds, and sunshine, all this renders the enjoyment of natural beauty a much more complex affair. It is less complete in that it has no strictly delimited object, but it has a different kind of completeness in that it presents its objects at the right time, in their right place, and under the right circumstances.

It may be that I am describing here a quality of living that is increasingly lacking in urbanized society. If aestheticians took on a larger social function, it might be to recommend a life of increased ritual at appropriate times. It is too much to expect a return to the celebration of the Church's year with its different coloring, literal and figurative, for Easter, Whitsun, and Christmas; but a life lived without changes according to season and recurrent occasions is immensely impoverished. In any event, I take my work to include the examination of the aesthetic quality of all kinds of experiences, as well as the formal enjoyment of the beauties of art and nature, and to note the variety within each range. What must be said, for example, of myth and fairy story, which are neither natural objects nor to be evaluated by the critical standards of literature? I doubt whether anyone can recall or feel at all interested by a discussion of "Cinderella" as the story was first presented to him. Nevertheless it is just as much a part of our cultural heritage as is *Hamlet*. I count nothing outside the range of my inquiry which complements or supplements the imaginative life of men, and I hope that the austerity of my formal requirements may make up for the laxity in content.

CHAPTER II

What Is a Work of Art?

Before proceeding to the amplification and carrying out of our program as outlined in Chapter I, we must give an account of the objects whose existence gives rise to our whole inquiry—that is to say, works of art. At first sight, to ask what is a work of art seems to be posing an academic question. As the inquiry proceeds however, the necessity for posing the question and the difficulties in answering it become increasingly clear. It is hoped that the examination will provide a starting point for aesthetic inquiry generally, which to begin with, at any rate, will arouse no dispute.

A claim for general agreement such as Clive Bell's "The starting point for all systems of aesthetics must be the personal experience of a peculiar emotion,"[1] is countered by I. A. Richards' "the phantom aesthetic state,"[2] and any attempt to claim beauty as the central concept is straight away confused by the varied contexts in which "beauty" and "beautiful" may function. We hear much more

[1] *Art,* London, 1914. P. 6.
[2] *Principles of Literary Criticism,* London, 1925. Title of Ch. 2.

often of a "beautiful stroke" in cricket than in
painting, and many of our moral judgments have
an aesthetic flavor. An action may be bold, dash-
ing, mean, underhanded, unimaginative, cringing,
fine, as well as right or wrong. Aesthetic adjectives
and adverbs may occur in any context, and part of
our job is to separate out the various uses and establish their interrelationships.

Even if we confine our attention to discourse
about art, we find a bewildering variety in the application of aesthetic terms. A critical judgment
may be upon the properties of a work of art considered as a sensible object, upon the artist's handling of his material, upon the ideas he is expressing in his work, or upon the degree of success with
which he communicates those ideas. Some critical
judgments resemble moral judgments upon the artist and the importance of his ideas. A work may be
described as slipshod, insincere, trivial, meretri-
cious, or as a shirking of the artist's problem. A
critic may distinguish between aspects and praise a
work under one aspect, "Good theater, but negligible as drama." Judgment may be upon the performers, judged in as many ways as was the composer or playwright, with the added complication
that the performer is an intermediary between artist and audience and must be judged in this capac-
ity too. ("What possessed this fine and subtle in-
terpreter of German song to present the most
aristocratic of Mozart's characters as a Prussian offi-
cer in a bad temper?") Our material is not only
talk about works of art, but also artists' opinions
upon their own work and that of their fellows, and

both artists and critics mix their critical opinions with aesthetic theory more or less well worked out. Much aesthetic theory is misleading because artists in words are generally able to give more complete account of their problems and intentions than are painters, sculptors, and composers.

Discourse about works of art is further complicated by the relationship of natural objects to paintings, sculptures, and literary works of art. Much critical and aesthetic argument has been engaged with the question of representation in art and of the suitability of aesthetic experience that has a flavor of natural feeling towards natural objects. Some aesthetic theories neglect the artist and take the object as given, treating it as if it might have come into existence without human agency. Others are based upon the relation of artist to spectator, still others upon the relation of the artist to his world, but it is rare to find any attempt at justification for concentrating upon one aspect only of the complex situation, artist-making-object-for-human-enjoyment.

In this confusion of discourse at different levels, we have no generally accepted aesthetic principles to help us order our material. Critical pronouncements seem to assume principles, but principles are of limited application and by no means generally accepted. It is as if in moral philosophy we could not assume that truth speaking was right, and lying wrong, not because of variety of circumstance, but because the rightness or wrongness itself was still in question. If we take aesthetic experiences or situations as our starting point, we have to ask the

person having the experience or involved in the
situation why he is or is not enjoying the object,
natural or man-made. If he is unskilled in finding
reasons for his enjoyment he may mislead us by his
answer, but if he is more or less sophisticated he
will probably give us an answer in which aesthetic
theory is already involved, thus begging our question. If we begin with works of art, we can at least
be sure that we have some undisputed facts; without any doubt whatever, there are pictures hanging
on the walls of galleries, statues standing on pedes-
tals, dramatic performances, ballets, and operas in
theaters, and instrumentalists and singers performing in concert halls. These objects and performances have been made and prepared at great ex-
penses of time and money, and audiences and
spectators are equally ready to expend great effort
to look at and hear them. If we are troubled by the
question of entertainment versus aesthetic enjoyment, we can at least say that some of our objects
have been made and performed for aesthetic contemplation, some of our gallery-gazing, theater- and
concert-going population do so contemplate these
objects, and we may even go further and say that
aesthetic contemplation is the suitable reaction to
these objects. I want to go further still and say that
aesthetic contemplation is the normal reaction, in
the sense that the object will count as a failure if a
spectator looks at it and is not moved to contemplation.

I want to use the word "failure" because I think
that to perceive a work of art is an achievement,
and to track down the causes of the failure would

throw light on aesthetic experience. (We all of us know the experience of being unable to look properly at a picture or a play because of some personal idiosyncrasy. "I know *Lear* is a great play, but I can't sit through it; I am squeamish about physical cruelty.")

We now have a factual starting point in the sense that there are undoubtedly objects described as "works of art," and if there are "aesthetic experiences," some of them undoubtedly occur when a man of sensibility submits himself actively and receptively to one of these objects. We must notice, however, that "work of art" is neither an entirely descriptive nor an entirely appraisive phrase—it represents a preliminary appraisal. This can be shown by noticing that in some contexts it is an insult to say of a picture that it is a work of art and in others, a compliment. A friend of mine visiting a very house-proud old lady admired the little front parlor with the unfortunate words, "It is quite a little drawing room!" The old lady replied with extreme stateliness, "This *is* the drawing room." She was assuming the preliminary appraisal, drawing room, but would not have rejected further admiration, such as, it has a pleasant outlook, it gets the evening sun, and so on. Similarly, we might praise the painting of an amateur as "quite a work of art," meaning that he ought to send it to an exhibition. We should not, visiting the studio of an academy artist, use these words; he assumes the preliminary appraisal, and, like the old lady, will not reject further words of admiration. This is not, however, the end of the matter. On inspection of the picture, we might come to the opinion that the academician's assumption was unjustified. We have the expectation that established writers and painters will go on producing works of art, but there might come a moment when critics begin to say, "Mr. X is merely repeating himself," "Miss Y has written a typical Y'ish novel." How then, do pictures, plays, poems, novels, musical compositions, and so on become "works of art"?

In his *Aspects of the Novel*[3] E. M. Forster defines the novel, quoting M. Abel Chevalley, as "a fiction in prose of a certain extent." Mr. Forster specifies the extent. A novel, he says, is "any fictitious prose work over fifty thousand words." What other definition, he asks, "will fit *The Pilgrim's Progress, Marius the Epicurean, The Adventures of a Younger Son, The Magic Flute, The Journal of the Plague Year, Zuleika Dobson, Rasselas, Ulysses,* and *Green Mansions?*" I am not concerned with this definition of the novel, but with what Mr. Forster is obviously wishing to contrast with the novel. From our point of view, he is beginning *in mediis rebus;* he is distinguishing the established novel from established short stories, scientific treatises, histories, and travel books, not from *True under Trial, Gone With the Wind,* and *The Sorrows of Satan,* which also are "fictions in prose of a certain extent." He goes on to point out specific excellences of his examples, but he assumes before he begins that they are all works of art in the preliminary sense, that is, that they are worthy of serious critical

[3] *Aspects of the Novel,* London, 1927. P. 15.

attention. They are over all the hurdles—publisher, reviewers, critics, public; they now figure in courses in English Literature and are reprinted in the Oxford World's Classics, i.e., they have now become part of the tradition. "Novel" expresses this preliminary appraisal and "work of art" is an expression of exactly the same kind. It is the phrase for established works of all kinds—pictures, plays, novels, poems, and so on. In applying the concept we are not actually engaged in critical appraisal, but noting that the object is worthy of critical appraisal. We are marking off objects beneath serious attention from objects properly noticed by critics. "Works of art" distinguishes paintings in galleries from paintings used by manufacturers of chocolate boxes and birthday cards. It distinguishes films noticed by reviewers and short stories in collections from films and short stories that are noticed by nobody at all but seen and read by hundreds.

At this point I recall an indignant protest from one of my students who was not only an expert in the art of film making and its appreciation, but was also very much aware of the social duty of critics. She maintained very strongly that it was the duty of critics to exercise some kind of judgment upon those works that they ignore as beneath their notice. For those producers and editors who cater for the majority of film-goers and for the buyers of glossy magazines there is no kind of critical check on the quality of the goods they offer, and it is precisely those who need their interests guarded who are left out of account. This complaint was, I think, justified when it was made, but now that radio and television provide the bulk of the entertainment for the man-in-the-street, the programs are given more or less adequate critical attention. Now that practically everyone is seeing and hearing the same programs, it is possible to scrutinize them, whereas it would have been a hopeless undertaking with the thousands of B films and shoddy magazines.

One important question arises from this account of "work of art" considered as a term of preliminary appraisal. There are pictures in the basement of the Tate Gallery as well as on the walls and books collecting dust on library shelves. Are these to be considered as demoted from their status as works of art? Here I must confess to being on uncertain grounds; I do not know enough about the history of criticism to attempt an answer, but it seems to me that once a work of art has become established in the way described above, it may go in and out of fashion, but not cease to be a work of art. I cannot think that critics interested in the art of painting could be so completely blind to the painterly qualities of the works they praise as their own account of their reasons leads us to believe. Victorian critics who were fascinated by the vividness, incident, and detail and by the story-telling power of the pictures must have accepted these pictures as worthy of serious consideration as pictures, even though they then went on to talk about them as if it were other qualities that mattered. I can more easily believe that they gave a misleading account of their reasons for liking pictures than that they never had an aesthetic experience when they looked at them.

This is borne out by the way works of art go in

and out of fashion. What changes is not the painterly qualities of the pictures and our regard for
them, but the way in which these qualities are ob-
scured or underlined by our liking or disliking of
the qualities of the "vehicle." Victorian critics were
delighted and we are revolted by the long lines of
Edward Burne-Jones's damsels streaming down
staircases with lilies in their hands. The damsels
positively helped the Victorians to see and enjoy the
long lines of robes and lily stalks, but prevented
critics of later times. W. P. Frith is just now coming
back into fashion, but critics do not say, "Now we
see that the Victorians were right; the thing that
matters is the life-like qualities of the incident and
crowd scenes," but point out the painterly virtues
of "Derby Day" and "Paddington Station." The pictures always had these qualities and critics of the
time would not have bothered with them if those
qualities were lacking, but they took them for
granted and then talked about qualities that, from
our point of view, are irrelevant. Critics vary from
one period to another in the kinds of reasons they
give for their appreciation. When they concentrate,
as they tend to do today, upon the virtues proper
to each art, what they say is much nearer to what
aesthetic philosophers say, and so it seems to us
"truer" criticism.

In summation, the qualities that interest aestheticians vis-à-vis critics constitute a *sine qua non* for
works of art; objects lacking these qualities are not
worth critical attention. We might take as a parallel, reasons given for their selections by judges at a
flower show. It goes without saying that the plants

exhibited must be healthy—they would not be put
in if they were not. The judges take this for granted
and then go on to talk about shape and size of
bloom, truth of color, and so on. The most important quality, health of plant, is just not mentioned.
Nobody would show a plant that had not this essential, nobody would show a picture that lacked
the essential qualities of painting. Its extra qualities
qua novel, picture, play take it in and out of fashion, its basic quality qualifies it to go in and out of
fashion. Sometimes its "extra" qualities are estimated so highly that we overlook its lack of basic
quality. This is more likely to happen in the literary arts. I do not think we should say that a picture
was great but not a work of art, though we might
say that a novel was great but not a work of art.
Percy Lubbock goes so far as to say of *War and
Peace* that Tolstoy has wasted his subject, from the
point of view of producing a work of art;[4] I must
hasten to point out that this occurs in many pages
of praise for the vividness of the scenes and characters of the book. "Before the profusion of *War and
Peace* the question of its general form is scarcely
raised. It is enough that such a world should have
been pictured; it is idle to look for proportion and
design in a book that contains a world."[5] Nevertheless, the criticism has been raised, and we have an
example of a great novel which is not a work of
art. This will be anathema to the lovers of Tolstoy,
but only because they think "work of art" such a
high term of praise and like *War and Peace* so much

[4] *The Craft of Fiction*, London, 1921. P. 41.
[5] *Ibid.*, p. 27.

that they will withhold no term of praise from it. If Lubbock is right, we can give all the other terms of praise to it, but just not this one. Some critics do not agree with Lubbock's pronouncement and discover form in a more subtle and complex sense of the word in *War and Peace* and other works hitherto described as formless. There is also a tendency in contemporary literary criticism to emphasize the importance of the moral qualities of the work under discussion. "This is a good book, and by 'good' I mean good not in the aesthetic but the moral sense, which is far more important." This critic, however, would not be concerned with the book at all if it were not good in the aesthetic sense. The author would not succeed in conveying moral quality if he were not a good writer.

At this point, I wish to consider some objections which have been raised to my account so far. It is said rightly, that the appraisive character of "work of art" belongs to ordinary words such as "rose" and "cabbage." A gardener, looking around your garden in which every rosebush was a mass of bloom, might say, "You haven't got a rose here." There is a difference though; the gardener is withholding the name "rose" from your roses because they are not good specimens of their kind and he could specify the respects in which they fall short. "That is a rose" is informative as well as appraisive, but there is no "kind" in an important sense of which a work of art is a specimen, and "that is a work of art" is almost entirely uninformative. It is an uninformative expression in the same sense in which "that is a birthday present" is uninformative.

A friend of mine, noticing an odd-looking glass object in a big shop at Christmas time, asked the assistant what it was. She looked at it for a minute and then said, "It's a Christmas present, Madam," which left things just where they were before. There are more interesting parallels between the two expressions, but I need to use this notion in another connection, so will leave it for the moment.

It is also objected that the phrase "work of art" is confined to paintings and sculptures, and that no one refers to novels, plays, poems, and musical compositions as works of art. It is true that the phrase is not used in this context, but the concept is. We use "works" of writings and compositions in the same appraisive way. If we say "the works of X" we feel that X ought to be the name of a considerable author or composer. The important difference between pictures and sculptures on the one hand and literary and musical works on the other is that artists and sculptors literally make the object with their own hands and place it before the public, while writers and composers give instructions for placing the object before the public. A man making a collection of valuable literary and musical objects would be using the concept "work of art," though he might never use the phrase.

We are now able to propose a tentative definition of a work of art. It is a picture, play, poem, etc., which has reached the public, been pronounced favorably upon by competent critics, and is now considered to be part of the tradition of English literature, French painting, and so on. We have proposed, further, that it has reached this position by the excellence peculiar to it in its medium, though it may be valued highly for its human interest. This is more likely to be true of literature and painting. Many apparent differences of opinion may be traced to this double evaluation. Some critics and philosophers of art wish to use "work of art" to refer exclusively to works displaying formal excellence and confine "aesthetic experience" to the thrill of recognition of form. These people look on the total work, with its insight into human nature, its richness and variety, as the vehicle of form and ask only that our attention shall not be distracted from form. Roger Fry,[6] speaking of Rembrandt, praises his sublime psychological imagination and the supreme quality of his plastic construction. He then goes on to say, "I do not know whether the world would not have gained had Rembrandt frankly divided his immoderate genius into a writer's and a painter's portion and kept them separate. We should thus be spared a clash of interests which leads our attention from one aspect to the other." Vernon Lee speaks of the representational element in painting as a useful relaxation from the effort of contemplating form.[7] Its only criterion of usefulness is that it should confine our attention within the frame and bring it back to the formal aspect, refreshed. It is, of course, more usually held that the tension of competing interests and their mutual reinforcement are just what make a Rembrandt picture satisfying. This leads me to my second proposal.

This is, that we should define "work of art" as a

[6] *Transformations*, London, 1926. Pp. 21, 22.
[7] *The Beautiful*, 3rd ed., London, 1917. P. 118.

conjunction of named particulars, i.e., it is the *Odyssey*, *Oedipus Rex*, "The Virgin of the Rocks," the Brandenburg Concertos, or . . . through an indefinite list. We should then be able to satisfy both kinds of critics. Each work is in the list through its own merit, not by being a good specimen, for it need conform to no rules. All that we need ask is that it should continue to win delighted contemplation and lend itself to growing knowledge. "This is a work of art" implies "Look, listen, attend carefully, you will find it worthwhile." The intermediate concepts between "this" and "work of art" are useful only as directing attention to certain features of the individual object and setting our attention in a certain way. Sometimes, indeed, the concepts may be a hindrance; we are prevented from receiving the full impact by looking with conceptually aroused expectations.

I want to emphasize the individuality of each work of art because I want to make room for both kinds of enjoyment. I sympathize with the austere delight of the formalist; it is difficult to achieve, but once experienced, it sets a standard that can never be forgotten. It might happen three or four times in a lifetime, and then not always in more than one art form. Those who have experienced it in one art form tend to think that it belongs especially to that art, not realizing that for others the situation may be reversed. It seems to be most easily achieved in music, with the most difficulty in literature. On the other hand, I sympathize with the delight in the richness and variety of the human interest in many great plays, poems, novels, and paintings. When people say that every detail matters, every quality is essential, we know what they mean. There is a close parallel here between the individuality of a work of art and a human being. One of P. G. Wodehouse's young men, trying to persuade his mean and curmudgeonly uncle to invite his friend to stay, says, "You'll like Ronnie Fish —he's got an aunt in the looney bin." The uncle says, "Is that supposed to be a reason for liking him?" Of course the nephew is not doing anything so silly as offering a reason for liking his friend. Any one of the qualities of his friend reinstates for him the delightful whole upon which he delights to dwell. This is the way in which we dwell upon the delightful whole of the play or novel, thinking of each feature in turn and willing to let go of none, though not allowing the detail to obscure the whole. Neither the person nor the play is "an" anything at all, and we are continually discovering new features which belong to the individual but not in accordance with any concept.

We may now attempt a classification of works of art, not into kinds, but into groups that will help us in our analysis of critical discourse. Works of art are either

1. Things made by the artist's own hand and placed before the public, e.g., pictures and statues. These are "works of art" in the ordinary sense of the term.

2. Instructions for placing the object before the public, e.g., musical scores, scripts of plays, novels, poems, etc. These fall into two categories. Musical scores and scripts give instruc-

tions for making an ephemeral object, a performance that must be repeated every time we wish to "have" the object. A relatively permanent object may be made, in accordance with the instructions, a recording that needs only mechanical skill to produce the performance. This, of course, will be one interpretation of the script or score by a given cast or set of instrumentalists. Blueprints, although they give instructions for making a permanent object, may belong to the first category.

3. (a) Performances of plays, ballets, musical compositions.

(b) Performances in which the performers are not carrying out the instructions of any other artist, e.g., clowns, acrobats, some dancers.

4. (a) Things made for some useful end or some end other than contemplation, but which nevertheless arouse delighted contemplation.

(b) Performances carried on for some end other than contemplation, but nevertheless arouse it, e.g., sports, military tattoos, ritualistic ceremonies.

Several problems arise here in connection with one or other of our categories. Our first heading is relatively straightforward, the only problem arising in connection with prints and copies of paintings and copies and casts of statues. A copyist may be regarded as taking the picture or statue as a model for the making of another object, and he might be a draftsman or an artist appreciating the work of another so completely that he re-creates it. The copies and prints may be regarded as tokens of the same type among themselves, but it is difficult not to give the original a different status. It has a privileged position in that it sets the standard by which the others are judged as more or less adequate reproductions.

Some philosophers object that the difference between an original painting or sculpture and prints and casts taken from them is important only because the technique of reproduction is as yet imperfect. It is a mere matter of fact, they argue, that copies are not indistinguishable from their originals. This seems ridiculous to most people who feel that somehow or another the peculiar methods of the artist must be recognizable in the painting—that if he has worked with bold strokes, somehow or another this must be evident—not to be simulated by any mechanical process which would lack the fire or the sensitivity or . . . This may be merely a romantic illusion, but we must wait and see!

A connected but more difficult problem arises in connection with performances. There is no difficulty in regarding Shakespeare's manuscript of *Hamlet* and all other copies as tokens of the same type. As contrasted with paintings, the original has only historical interest, copyists needing nothing but the ability to read and write and the power of concentration upon the original words and care in reproducing them. When it comes to performances, we have a problem of quite a different kind. Performances are judged as better or worse than one another even though we have no standard against which to measure them. Critics sometimes appear to assume that the performance that comes closest to the playwright's intention is the best, and when he is still living, or has approved a performance within living memory, then we might be able to claim a certain performance as standard. Nicolas Nabokov, writing on the Moscow Art Theater says, "Fortunately, or unfortunately, I belong to a generation that saw Chekhov's plays at the Moscow Art Theater in what was largely the original cast, and these performances became for me a kind of Platonic model." On the other hand, not all playwrights and composers are the best interpreters of their own work, not all poets the best readers of their own poems. The various performances might each better be regarded as a work of art in its own right, Olivier's *Hamlet,* Pavlova's *Dying Swan,* Beecham's *Figaro* appearing in our list of named particulars. The copyists make their appearance as lesser performers modeling themselves on the artists of stage and orchestra.

Playwrights differ in their view of the functions of actors and producers. There is the dramatist who, by every means in his power, tries to insure that nothing shall be left to the actor's own initiative. For him, the business of the producer is simply to place the play before the audience with no interposition of personality. George Bernard Shaw, with his minute stage directions, is a dramatist of this kind. Others look on the actors as collaborators and the script as incomplete—the work of art coming into existence with each performance. Composers are similarly divided; some tend to think of instrumentalists as a mere means of giving the music to the audience, some going so far as to claim that the sound produced by instrumentalists, while charming and delightful, is not essential to the appreciation of music except for the musically illiterate. Some architects claim that the blueprint is the work of art, and the building the work of craftsmen.

The modern notion of staging "happenings" and inviting, even demanding, the cooperation of the audience in chanting, moving, shouting, and so on, is apparently only an extension of the belief that the play, opera, or concert is incomplete until it is performed before an audience. The essence of the modern view is that there is to be no "object" that it is the duty of the artist to present and that of the audience to take, but only a set of stimuli to induce a state of free and uninhibited emotion. It is not even clear that the aim is to produce a common emotion—it is rather each member of the combined cast-audience having his own experience, doing his own thing. There are even theories according to which painters are engaged in a similar enterprise. Speaking of the work of Olle Baertling, described as "the creator of open form," Teddy Brunius says, "He aims at annihilating the technical surface, eliminating the painting as a material object: his surfaces of color become like stretched membranes, which we sense only as vibrations; his pointed 'triangles' are not geometric figures but figures of force, figures of a particular intensity, a particular charge of waxing or waning displacements."[8] Baertling himself speaking of his discussions on art with Auguste Herbin, says, "Our discussions certainly stimulated my efforts to create multidimensional effects, or rather an absence of dimension, by eliminating the background. Background, I argued, was a naturalistic burden which Herbin would also be happy to abandon."[9] First the frame has gone, then the background, and finally the painting itself "considered as a material object." This may be compared to the disappearance of the conventional stage, followed by the removal of the "distance" between actor and audience.

No matter what view architects may take of the function of master builders, there is no doubt that buildings as well as furniture, pottery, and carpets are pleasing objects and are sometimes described as beautiful. They are "works of art" if our criterion is that we should delight in their look. But there is an important difference between the work of artists and that of craftsmen. Objects made for use are judged by a double standard, one connected with their adaptation to their use and one connected with their look. This may not be decisive. The tension between competing criteria of look and use may give aesthetic satisfaction; the teapot must look as if it will pour out well *and* pour out well. For me, however, the decisive difference is that craft objects are not importantly individual. It would be sensible to ask craftsmen

[8] *Baertling, Creator of Open Form*, Stockholm, 1969. P. 57.
[9] *Ibid.*, p. 34.

making a chair to make us another just like it, but not a painter painting a picture. We could ask him to paint another picture, but we should have to wait and see what it was like. It is no accident that craft objects cannot figure in our list of named objects. Any chair of Chippendale's best period will do; there is a tradition of English furniture making, but it is bound up with a way of living, and part of our enjoyment derives from the realization that there were fortunate people who sat upon Chippendale chairs every day. If they had never been used, but made especially for a museum, they would be different objects.

Our discussion of craft objects is complicated by some cases that fall between and seem to come from both sides. There are artists whose work leads to such critical comment as "this is the efficient orchestration of a triviality," "as near perfect theater work as it is possible to imagine," "technical perfection, but the artist has nothing to say." From the side of craft, some objects fulfill their end with such mastery that they take their place among the classics of literature. Newton's *Principia* is so well written that it might appear on our list, and some detective stories come out of their category of wit-exercising writings and rank as novels.

Processes and objects of aesthetic appraisal may be of several kinds. If someone is cutting out a frock with barely enough material, but by twisting and turning the pattern, gets it with hardly a snippet over, we might say "That was quite a work of art." We should not say it if the cutter-out was simply economizing. In praising the performance, we are not concerned with the movements of the performer nor with the product, but simply with the neat and ingenious adaptation of means to end. On the other hand, what we usually describe as an "artist" in dressmaking is one who, with great slashings of the scissors and with no regard for waste, makes an object that is pleasing in itself and in relation to a particular person and a particular occasion. There are performances in which the performer is simply placing the work of another artist before us, but we may also value their work as good in its own right. There are finished performances of bad plays as well as productions that faithfully render the work of the playwright.

There is another important class of aesthetically pleasing performances in which the performers are not carrying out the instructions of another artist but are acting spontaneously. Star performers in ice hockey, cricket, football, and sports generally are valued almost as much for their elegance in action as for their run-making and goal-getting ability. (The elegant batsman, however, like the teapot must not only look as though he will make runs but actually make them.) Sports commentators use the terms of aesthetic appraisal as freely as do art critics; footballers are described as "intuitive artists," "inspired clowns," and there is the general run of "good solid craftsmen."

We may notice, further, that critics make their names in connection with the work of particular artists, even with particular works, and not with poetry, painting, or the drama in general. If we want to follow the advice of a drama critic, it is

more important to know which particular plays he
appreciates than what his views on drama are. We
might allow him one or two blind spots, but he
must be sound on most of the great plays.

In this chapter I have not been concerned with
the requirements that people in general assume for
giving the title "work of art," "artist," to things,
processes, and people. These requirements vary with
the implicit aesthetic theories assumed at various
times. Sometimes they refer to the way in which
the artist works and the way in which the work was
produced. When asked whether the chimpanzee
Congo's pictures were "works of art," almost every
unsophisticated person answered that they could
not be since a chimpanzee is not capable of expressing his experiences. Some added a further reason, that Congo cheated, or rather someone cheated
on his behalf, by giving him the brushes already
filled with paint and taking away his canvas when
it was judged he had done enough to it. Rocks
and stones worn by wind and rain so that they
look like a piece by Henry Moore are similarly refused the title "work of art." In both these cases,
sophisticated people tend to say that it entirely depends on the look—if Congo's paintings look well,
they may be works of art and so may weather-
worn rocks.

The uncovering of the grounds for such opposed
opinions reveals assumptions as to the nature of
art, the essential features of creative activity and
of the artist *qua* artist, of aesthetic experience
and aesthetic value. These are assumptions that
need to be brought out into the open, and in the

succeeding chapters I hope to provide the context in which they are held and determine how far they are to be accepted or rejected.

At this point the inquiry leads us in two directions, one into the nature of the objects held to be valuable and the other into the nature of the experience that may give rise to such evaluation and in which their value is held to consist. If we were to ask ourselves the question, "What are the aesthetically valuable objects possessed by the modern world?" we should answer first, "The objects described above." But suppose the art galleries were locked or there was nobody who cared to enter them, our people blind to the beauties of architecture and nature; is there anything aesthetically valuable in the world at all? We are led to wonder whether it is the objects enumerated above or the experiences enjoyed in their presence which are the "valuable things."

Another question arises here: Is the value of the experience to be defined in terms both of its own qualities and of the qualities of the object towards which it is felt, or does its value lie only in its own qualities so that it does not matter to what it is directed? Suppose a city in which there were Nash terraces, Wren churches, galleries full of Rembrandts, Leonardos, Van Goghs, and Constables and people gazing enraptured at mud, stones, and dirt. Is anything aesthetically valuable going on in that city? I hope to show that the worth of an experience is to be matched by the worth of the object, and moreover to convince my readers.

CHAPTER III

Aesthetic Experiences and Attitudes

As was said above, there are now two directions in which our inquiry might move, toward an examination of the beautiful objects of nature and art or of the state which their contemplation induces in the beholder. However, what is said of the one will have a bearing upon what is said of the other, the difference lying in the placing of the emphasis. Modern thinkers have tended to place the emphasis on the experience. This, I think, is largely because the art of many different times and places has become available to us. This means that we can no longer look to the historical-geographical environment for clues as to the intention of the artist or to the demands of the community. We simply have the objects and our reaction to them. It is no accident that Clive Bell, who gives us our starting point, was deeply moved by the art of the Far and Middle East, Chinese pottery, and Persian rugs. His credo is embodied in the dictum, "There is no doubt that aesthetic theory must take its starting point in the personal experience of a peculiar emo-

tion."[1] This is an extremely odd statement. First,
the "personal experience." Any experience is personal in the sense that it is felt by a person. Clive
Bell must be wishing to emphasize that in the case
of aesthetic emotion one can know what it is only
by one's own experience and not by hearsay. It is
conceivable that we might understand what anger
was by seeing other people in a rage even though
we ourselves never felt angry, but there is no way
to behave that would give other people a clue as
to the nature of aesthetic experience except standing and gazing. (Of course, there is talk about enjoyment of aesthetic objects, but this would be enlightening only between people already having
had the experience.)

Now, a "peculiar emotion." "Peculiar" here cannot
mean odd or strange, but uniquely appropriate—but
appropriate to what? Not to itself—this would be
meaningless. It must be appropriate to its object,
and now we see why the experience was described
as personal. It is not only that the emotion is to
be felt by a person, but by *this* person in the presence of *this* object to which the emotion is peculiarly appropriate. Clive Bell tells us what it is about
the object that makes it able to arouse the peculiar
emotion: it is its possession of "significant form."
We may now reformulate Bell's dictum: aesthetic
theory can be discovered only by someone who
has himself had an experience of recognizing significant form in a particular object with the appropriate
aesthetic thrill. It will not be enough to have had

[1] *Art,* London, 1914. P. 6.

the thrill, nor to recognize significant form; the two must occur together and be mutually appropriate. Of course, there will be odd occasions such as hurrying through a gallery and catching sight of a picture that one knows will be exciting if looked at properly. We could even recognize hurriedly the presence of significant form, but not allow ourselves the time to experience the thrill. This would not count against Bell's theory.

The modern preoccupation with aesthetic experience dates from the eighteenth-century philosophical thinkers who, in their concern with questions of morals and politics, and with the example of the great success of the mathematical sciences, wished to base their own studies just as firmly. Mathematical truth did not seem to them to be questionable, and they sought just as firm a foundation for morals and politics. David Hume thought that in his laws of the association of ideas, he had uncovered and formulated a principle that would be just as unquestionable and fruitful as Newton's law of the attraction of gravitation among all material particles. He and his fellow thinkers therefore thought they should first pose the question, "How do we know, how can we be sure?" and answer it by uncovering the elements and the principle of their association. Their answer was therefore in terms of the fundamental facts, "the ideas"; not "I see a horse," but "I see a brown shape, hear a neighing noise, and by custom learn to say 'I see a horse.'" When they began to be interested in questions of beauty and taste, then they thought the first question to be raised was as to the origin of our ideas of the beautiful and the sublime and what in our experience is the foundation both of underlying agreements and variations in taste.

Anyone interested in aesthetic theory—that is to say, anyone who thinks art and beauty and their appreciation are worthy of study—must be interested for one of the following reasons and must hold one of the following beliefs. First, the beautiful objects of nature and art are so valuable that he studies their characteristics for the sake of the objects alone. This is not a reference to critics of painting, music, literature, etc. These people certainly think that the characteristics of works of art are worthy of study, but each one is concerned with his own particular art. The aesthetician is concerned not with the marks of excellence in painting, literature, etc., but with what makes *these* marks, marks of excellence in general. Or second, he must think the experience of these beautiful objects is so beneficial, either to the community or to the individual, that the objects must be studied from the point of view of determining which of their qualities fit them for fulfilling this end. Or third, he may think the experience so valuable in itself that it needs to be examined and the qualities of the object bringing it about correlated with its features. This was the belief of the "Bloomsbury Set"—their philosopher G. E. Moore including "the admiring contemplation of beauty" as one of the values of civilized living.[2]

People holding the first belief may look on the beautiful object as valuable simply because of its

[2] *Principia Ethica*, Cambridge, 1903. Pp. 188 ff.

own nature or because it is the sign of some reality beyond itself. Plato and Aristotle agreed in finding the objects delightful, but both were concerned solely with their influence on the character of the beholders and, more importantly, through the beholders, with the benefit to the community. Plato's description of the objects of art was unfavorable on both counts. Natural objects were simply imitations of the truly real, and the objects of art, still worse, were imitations of those imitations, and our enjoyment of them a counterfeit emotion. Consequently, the influence of art on the human character is bad, and this badness is reflected in the life of the community. Aristotle disagreed. For him, art was not only pleasing, but also beneficial in its effects, both on the individual and on the community. His *Poetics* consists of an analysis, chiefly of tragedy, to show how the elements of tragedy are such as to bring about the good end.

In medieval theory the beautiful things of nature were thought of as symbols of God's power and goodness and of his concern for his creatures. Consequently, works of art were attempts to show men the symbolic nature of the real things. Favorite words for describing beautiful things were "clarity" and "radiance," this choice of words showing that the importance of art was held to lie more in what it symbolized than in what it was—or what it appeared to be.

In modern theory the assumption is that the aesthetic state is intensely satisfying, valuable in itself, of its own kind, and the most important element in the total aesthetic situation for philosophical study. Art is justified because this valuable state can be brought about in no other way. If it could be shown that this valuable state *could* be brought about in some other way—say, by taking drugs, or self-hypnosis by chanting, moving, or swaying with one's fellows—then art would be expendable. This is the weakness inherent in any aesthetic theory placing the main emphasis on the value of the aesthetic state.

I. A. Richards, while largely agreeing with this modern emphasis on the aesthetic state, questions one of its assumptions. His second chapter in *Principles of Literary Criticism* is headed "The Phantom Aesthetic State."[3] For him there is no such thing as *the* aesthetic emotion. He says that there is no difference in kind between our experience as we walk to the National Gallery and our experience inside when we are actually looking at the pictures. There is a difference, of course, or rather I should say there are differences between the two total states; as we walk in the street there are thousands of things impinging on our eye and ear, many trains of ideas, thoughts, emotions starting up and trailing away without coming to any satisfactory kind of ending. We are in a state of chaos and confusion and obtaining no satisfaction from what is going on before our eyes. A work of art, a painting, a poem, a play is so constructed that what we see and hear leads us to something that is suited to it, rounds it off, brings order out of chaos and yields a satisfying experience. T. E. Hulme goes so far as to

[3] *Principles of Literary Criticism*, London, 1925. Title of Ch. 2.

describe music as imposing some kind of musical harmony even upon our chaotic and discordant experience.[4]

The question as to the uniqueness of an emotion is a difficult one to answer, and I do not think that Richards has even embarked upon the way to an answer. He has opposed a complex emotional state to what Clive Bell has described as "a thrill," which I think cannot be complex, at least not a complex of emotions, though it might be a reaction to a complex object. Bell is not speaking of the long process by which we reach fuller awareness of a work of art. I think his "thrill" is probably the first intimation that here is something worthy of study, as well as, finally, the recognition of the achievement of full awareness. It is more a climax and a preliminary warning of something terrific, and there is no reason at all why the state that Richards describes should not come in between. What Richards really wishes to dispute is the occurrence of this immediately recognizable, unanalyzable shock of delight. Perhaps he simply does not feel it, and if so, there is no point in trying to convince him. If someone stubbornly denies that another person feels an emotion of which he himself has no experience, there is nothing to be done about it. My only qualm here is that Richards so obviously delights in poetry, and feels all that ought to be felt about it, that it seems extremely unlikely that he is missing the essential element in aesthetic experience. I think he must be so obsessed with the valuable

[4] *Speculations,* London, 1936. Pp. 21–22.

total experience that he just will not accept the sudden shock that perhaps acts as a catalytic agent.

One can speak only as one finds, and I commit myself to the side of the aesthetic thrill. I have experienced it very rarely in my life, but once is enough. The odd part is that it seems to me attainable in music, which is not "my" art. For Bell it seems to have occurred chiefly in painting, and it may be that Richards, who is obviously moved more by poetry than by any other art, misses it for that reason. One tends to think of it as belonging chiefly to the art where one first experienced it, but it is probably attainable in any. One tends to think that one's own art is peculiarly fitted to yield the highest experience, but there are different kinds of enjoyment of art. There is the rich, full, evocative experience of literature and the high, austere recognition of the beauty of a Chinese vase. I must not leave the impression that the genuine aesthetic thrill cannot be achieved in literature. Form is much harder to achieve and to recognize in the "richer" arts— literature and representational painting. We may recall Roger Fry's astounding judgment on Rembrandt, quoted above.[5] What Fry has overlooked is the possibility of form *in* content and not as opposed to content, e.g., the "pairs" of lovers in Shakespearean comedy and the pairs, say, in *Middlemarch*—Dorothea and Mr. Casaubon, Rosamond and Lydgate.

I have not said that aesthetic experience is pleasant. Of all the spheres in which utilitarianism

[5] See Chapter 2, note 6.

is invoked, it is most inept in aesthetics. No one would wish to say that to see a performance of *Lear* was pleasant—immensely satisfying and worthwhile, but not pleasant. We would consent to say it was pleasant only if we were forced to choose between "pleasant" and "distasteful." Every possible experience one can imagine has an accompaniment of pleasure-pain, from the faintest suspicion to an intense anguish or delight. We are saying nothing of any importance about any experience when we say it was or was not "pleasant."

Perhaps I should have referred earlier to A. G. Baumgarten,[6] who in 1750 coined the title *Aesthetica* for a study he was proposing to inaugurate but which turned into something different as he worked. First of all, his study was to have been of what he called "inferior cognition." He was to do for sense perception what logicians had done for reasoning. For this science, *aesthetica,* coming from the Greek *aisthētikos,* sense perception, would have been a suitable title. What his treatise turned into was the study of aesthetic feeling. Perhaps this is just as it should be. We may find that our enjoyment of beauty is the enjoyment of "perfected perception," giving keenest delight. This is one of the reasons that I do not entirely like the emphasis upon experience in aesthetic study. Unless experience is correlated point by point with the quality of the object, one may be said to be enjoying oneself in the presence of the object rather than enjoying the object. It may be very pleasant to sit and day-

[6] *Aesthetica,* Frankfurt, 1758. Part 1, Part II.

dream while the orchestra makes pleasant sounds, but that is not to enjoy the music. To fail to insist upon the correlation with the qualities of the object is to risk falling into the modern heresy of thinking that it is the state that is important, and that it does not matter how you got there. I once had a dream in which I was in a station waiting room and Groucho Marx was the porter, sweeping out the room with his efficient inefficiency, keeping up a running fire of Groucho conversation. In the morning I remembered a hilarious occasion but none of the jokes. It kept me happy all the morning, but it was not an appreciation of Groucho's humor because none of this was present to me. Being kept happy without the reinstatement of the object is not the enjoyment of art. When the poet says, "Full many a flower is born to blush unseen and waste its sweetness on the desert air," he is saying not only that its sweetness is being wasted but that its qualities are being unperceived. We might look on Kant as combining Baumgarten's two tasks. Kant, too, used "aesthetics" for the name of the analysis of sense perception and later in *The Critique of Judgment* for the discovery of the laws of feeling, not in the sense of causal, psychological laws, but the laws of the appropriateness of feeling.

To revert to Clive Bell once more and to Richards' objections, we have to recognize that there are thousands of delighted perceptions, ranging from what is as nearly simple as anything can be to that of the most complex of the arts. Bell's thrill of delight might be evoked by a field of poppies blazing in the sunlight. One might say, "I never knew what scarlet was before," but there is no complexity here and so no form. It is as simple as any experience can be, but I think belonging to the category of aesthetic delight nevertheless. There is a whole range from the simple pleasure in a musical sound or a color, through all the degrees of appreciation of natural beauty and art, to the highest pitch of complete and delighted awareness of a complex object.

Another feature of aesthetic experience and of the aesthetic attitude in modern theory is what Edward Bullough called "distance." He says, "Distance . . . is obtained by separating the object and its appeal from one's own self, by putting it out of gear with practical needs and ends. Thereby the 'contemplation' of the object becomes alone possible. But it does not mean that the relation between the self and the object is broken to the extent of becoming 'impersonal.' Distance does not imply an impersonal, purely intellectually interested relation. . . . On the contrary, it describes a personal relation, often highly emotionally coloured, but of a *peculiar character.* Its peculiarity lies in that the personal character of the relation has been, so to speak, filtered. . . . The events and characters of the drama . . . appeal to us like persons and incidents of normal experience, except that that side of their appeal, which would usually affect us in a directly personal manner, is held in abeyance."[7]

[7] " 'Psychical Distance' as a Factor in Art and an Aesthetic Principle," in *Aesthetics,* ed. Elizabeth M. Wilkinson, London, 1954. P. 96.

The interesting thing about this concept is that it found immediate acceptance as though it needed only to be pointed out. Until the advent of the more recently formed theories of involvement it had never been questioned. The concerned and articulate young reject the whole notion of contemplation as almost frivolous in the face of the happenings in the real world. The theory of audience participation has reached the pitch of anti-theory. Actors and audience participate not in the production of a work of art, but in what is meant to be a spontaneous expression of feeling. It is hard to understand how people holding these views can put themselves into drama schools, hire halls, and take the stage. What are they supposed to be doing if they are not professional performers?

To return to the notion of distance, we may ask what difficulties in the theory of art appreciation it is supposed to meet. It precisely delineates the kind of enjoyment in which we may be said equally to "enjoy" a performance of *Lear* and of an Oscar Wilde comedy. At one end of the scale is the cold awareness, "over-distanced" as Bullough would say, of a scenic designer looking with professional interest at a performance of *A Midsummer Night's Dream*. At the other end of the scale there is the passionate self-identification of a jealous husband with Othello, in this case "under-distanced." "Tragedy trembles always on the knife edge of a *personal* reaction," as Edward Bullough says.[8] The balance is a state of exquisite awareness, neither the cold

8 "Psychical Distance," p. 112.

contemplation of a mere observer nor the passionate warmth of a partisan.

The notion of distance is easily misunderstood. Eric Shorter says of Jean Genet's play *The Blacks,* ". . . every time the show looks like getting up steam the author snuffs it out or interrupts the action on the principle (Brechtian?) that distance between the actors and audience should be encouraged." This seems to me to be the antithesis of the notion of distance. Brecht was very anxious to counteract the self-deception of fashionable audiences wallowing in emotion and supposing themselves to be most sensitively aware of the ills of the world when they were really indulging themselves in an orgy of sentimentality about the fate, say, of Marguerite. He set himself firmly to demonstrate over and over again that what was being presented to them was a stage performance. He managed this by making obvious the tricks of stage effects, by displaying the artificial and conventional methods of making the effects, and sometimes by having his actors address the members of the audience directly. This device is effectively used in comedy, but Brecht used it in tragedy as well. In a film of the Marx Brothers, Chico is about to play the piano. Groucho steps to the front and says to the audience, "Why don't you go out and have a quick one? I've got to stay here." This is allowable because in some kinds of comedy the relation between actor and audience is a personal one. We are enjoying Groucho and not merely the film, but in tragedy the effect is to destroy distance; it is to involve us as persons with the persons playing the personages. It may be objected that I am confusing the actor with the person he is presenting, but that is the very point. To show the personage, say, Hamlet as being played by Olivier is to draw us into a connection with Olivier-Hamlet. I am not saying that this is not what Brecht wanted to do, but that it is a mistake to think of it as encouraging distance.

The reference to Brecht introduces a new and very difficult notion, that of illusion. What Brecht has been at pains to destroy is dramatic illusion, which has been taken for granted at times, as the essence of art. We are sometimes told that painting is a matter of presenting three-dimensional objects on a two-dimensional canvas. If this really were the essence of art, it is difficult to see why it was worth doing. Professor E. H. Gombrich has given the answer conclusively in his *Art and Illusion*.[9] Art is illusory precisely in the sense, and in no other, that perception itself is illusory. Just as we hear in one sense "clip-clop clip-clop" and in another sense hear a horse going by, so in one sense we see a colored shape either in nature or in art and in another sense see a real woman in a red dress or a represented woman in a red dress in a picture. It might be thought that conjurers are illusionists if anybody is, but even they do not really put us under an illusion. I have heard people, speaking about a conjuring performance, say in a discontented tone, "He doesn't really saw a woman in half." It is difficult to know why they are discontented. It goes without saying that they do not want

9 *Art and Illusion*, London, 1960. Ch. III, Sect. i–iv; Ch. VIII.

the woman to be really sawed in half. Nevertheless they find the performance somehow dissatisfying. What they want, and what they have not been given, is illusion. There has been too much preparation, too much apparatus, opening and closing of boxes, thrusting rods through holes, and so on. What they have been given is an apparent demonstration that the conjurer could not wield the saw without sawing the woman in half. There has been a total lack of illusion. There is more of an illusion in a stage performance, because we are led imperceptibly into the time and place where the playwright wishes to have us. We give ourselves up willingly to the illusion—it is not exactly as Coleridge says that we suspend disbelief; it is rather that we give up the belief-disbelief attitude altogether.

The point of this digression is that in witnessing a work of art we willingly put ourselves under its influence, and this is what the earnest young people of the present day cannot forgive us. We are indulging ourselves in make-believe, almost as if we were taking drugs. It may be objected that these same young people think that it is perfectly suitable to take drugs, but if they were to consent to speak about their reasons, they would probably say that it was more honest simply to take drugs than to deaden our sense of what was wrong with the world by submitting ourselves to a world of make-believe.

There are several variations on the theme that submitting oneself to the world of art is wrong; this will be discussed more fully later, but at the moment we may merely notice that some accounts of the aesthetic experience make it subject to moral judgment, notably that of Tolstoy.[10] Tolstoy believed that art was justified only, or even that it was art only, if it brought about brotherly love among human beings, so that the enjoyment of the experience of art for its own sake is one of the worst forms of self-indulgence.

A peculiar form of the notion of aesthetic experience as a case of enjoying oneself in the presence of the object is the theory of empathy (*Einfühlung*). Theodor Lipps says, "Aesthetic satisfaction consists in this; that it is satisfaction in an object, which yet, just so far as it is an object of satisfaction, is not an object but myself; or it is satisfaction in a self which yet, just so far as it is aesthetically enjoyed, is not myself but something objective. This is what is meant by Empathy: that the distinction between the self and the object disappears or rather does not yet exist."[11]

Empathy is presented as a factual account of what as a matter of fact happens when a man becomes aware of and appreciates an aesthetic object. Of the followers of *Einfühlung*, Vernon Lee was the most determined to introduce these doctrines into English aesthetic theory. She began with a psychological account of aesthetic appreciation in terms of the projection of the muscular and organic sensations, i.e., of the real and remembered kin-

10 *What Is Art?* trans. Aylmer Maude, London, 1930. See especially Ch. IX and p. 275. See also E. H. Gombrich, *Meditations on a Hobby Horse*, London, 1963. Pp. 155–59.
11 "'Empathy,' Inward Imitation, and Sense Feeling," 1903. This appears in *Philosophies of Beauty*, trans. E. F. Carritt. P. 253.

esthetic sensation, into the perceived object—for example, she says that when we speak of a mountain rising, we are "transferring from ourselves to the looked-at shape of the mountain, not merely the thought of the rising, which is really being done by us at that moment, but the idea of rising as such which had been accumulating in our minds long before we ever came into the presence of that particular mountain."[12] Later Vernon Lee was converted by Karl Groos and Theodor Lipps to prefer the physiological account implicit in the quotation just given. Her point of view was reinforced by more or less contemporary accounts of architecture such as that of Geoffrey Scott in *The Architecture of Humanism.* He says, "A spire, when well designed, appears to soar; . . . so, too, by the same excellent mechanism of speech, arches 'spring,' vistas 'stretch,' domes 'swell,' Greek temples are 'calm,' and the Baroque façade is 'restless.' The whole of architecture is, in fact, unconsciously invested by us with human movements and human moods. . . . This is the humanism of architecture."[13] We may compare this with the following passage from Vernon Lee: "We attribute to lines, not only balance, direction, velocity, but also thrust, resistance, strain, feeling, intention, and character." She concludes that it is "the attribution of our vital modes, of our movement, conation, intention, will, and character to assemblages of lines and sounds that explains preference for certain forms rather than others; and this

12 *The Beautiful,* Cambridge, 1910. P. 65.
13 *The Architecture of Humanism,* London, 1914. Pp. 210 ff.

selection among visible and audible forms constitutes art."[14] Scott's statement is useful in that he himself was an artist and in examining an aesthetic theory we want to know what it is that the artist is supposed to be doing. Apparently he is using all that he knows of the powers of the various forms at once to excite and to calm by presenting us with the perfect "assemblages of lines and sounds," i.e., with the perfect object for aesthetic appreciation.

Theories of this type are typical of their time and of their recent past. Poets such as Wordsworth felt strongly the union of men with nature from both sides. Not only do we feel ourselves in harmony with nature, but we literally feel ourselves *in* nature. Moreover, natural objects are thought of as animate and as sharing human emotions. When Wordsworth says,

> *And 'tis my faith, that every flower*
> *Enjoys the air it breathes,*

he is speaking literally. To enjoy aesthetic experience is to become aware of this oneness with nature and to enjoy the emotions along with the emotions of the natural objects. The function of the artist is to make clear this oneness and bring about a unity embracing nature, the artist, and the spectator.

The further attraction for many thinkers of empathy and similar accounts is that they are presented as factual and are therefore to be tested by scientific investigation. This is what is said in words, but when we look more closely, the scientific na-

---

[14] *The Beautiful,* Cambridge, 1913. P. 142.

ture of such theories is seen to be more apparent than real. All that is being offered is a theory in terms of scientific sounding terms, such as "muscular contractions," "satisfaction of impulses," etc. I. A. Richards uses the term "synaesthesia," i.e., "a sensation produced at a point different from the point of stimulation: a sensation of another kind suggested by one experience (e.g., colour-hearing)."[15] (This is according to *Chamber's Twentieth Century Dictionary.*) Thus, the rich and satisfying nature of aesthetic experience lies in the power of the work of art to bring into awareness a host of related images and impulses so organized as to present a unity and to satisfy the impulses. The test of excellence in art, then, is in the number of related images that are evoked while still retaining their unity and harmony, and in the number of impulses that can be brought into harmonious play and satisfied. Now the only scientific feature of this account is that it uses the words "impulses" and "images" and invokes the notions of calling up by association, etc. There is no hint of any kind of scientific test that might be used in determining the excellent in art, and we may notice that in Richards' own very good *Practical Criticism* he uses the conceptual apparatus of the normal literary critic.

A further criticism of empathy as an account of aesthetic appreciation is that it applies only to what are called the "superior senses" of sight and hearing. V. Basch, who introduced the doctrine of *Einfühlung* into France, says explicitly that the aesthetic

[15] Charles Ogden, I. A. Richards, and James Wood, *Foundations of Aesthetics,* London, 1922. P. 78.

feelings arise only from the superior senses of hearing and sight and are not directly related to our organic functions.[16] It is easy to see that an empathic account of the pleasures of smell and taste would satisfy nobody. The only organic accompaniment of the contemplation of a dish, however exquisitely blended the flavors, would be the watering of the mouth in anticipation. Smell does nothing for anybody in anticipation. One could see an old-fashioned cabbage rose and feel sure that it would smell delightfully, but it would be evocative only of the dawning of a summer day in the past and of memories connected with such days. There is no doubt that scents are evocative in the sense of calling up the past. There is nothing more nostalgic than the scent of a certain kitchen connected with our childhood, let us say. On the other hand, aesthetic objects ought to give rise to a desire for increased acquaintance. There is nothing to be done about smells except to get more of them, and there is no variation to be expected within a long period of smelling. When Blake says,

> *He who binds to himself a Joy*
> *Doth the wingèd life destroy,*

this image suggests to me somebody with his nose buried in a clove carnation, smelling, smelling, and longing for something more but not knowing what.

As for tastes, gourmets assure us that the pleasure of a good dinner is aesthetic. One of the problems here is that in order to enjoy it we have literally to

[16] *Essai Critique sur L'Esthétique de Kant*, Paris, 1896. P. 283.

consume and so destroy the object. It is as if the
ardor of our gaze might destroy a picture as we enjoyed it. It is difficult here to know how far one is
being influenced by the literal spatial connections of
the distance metaphor. We may literally stand at a
distance from a picture and enjoy it, and Sir Ken-
neth Clark has described how it is possible to ap-
proach to a certain point and lose distance both
literally and metaphorically.[17] By coming very
near to the painting we are no longer looking at it
but studying a canvas covered with blobs and
streaks of paint. From being spectators we are becoming critics of technique, so that in changing our
physical position we are also changing our mental
attitude. Now in the case of gastronomy, there is
nothing corresponding to the physical distance except in the case of wine tasters and tea tasters who
do their best by not swallowing the wine or the tea.
This does not count, however, because they are
definitely taking up the attitude of critics and eval-
uating the various flavors. There is nothing whatever to do for the enjoyment of a good dinner but
to eat it. It is, of course, possible to eat it attentively,
distinguishing the various flavors combining to produce the over-all flavor, but this is a very poor kind
of taking up of distance. Moreover, we could simply
read the recipe.

We are left then with two possibilities. First, we
may believe that our senses of taste and smell provide genuine aesthetic experience; if so, we must
insist on different accounts for the "higher" and

[17] "Six Great Pictures. No. 3. 'Las Meniñas,' by Velás-
quez," in London *Sunday Times*, June 2, 1957.

"lower" senses. Second, we may believe that the senses of sight and sound provide the only experiences worthy of being called "aesthetic," and then we may consider the theory of empathy as a serious candidate for acceptance.

I say "*we* may believe" because I must impress on my readers that they are among the people who have the experiences validating or invalidating the theories of art critics and philosophers. They must look upon themselves not only as receptive to argument and discussion by people who have thought long and earnestly about such matters, but also as called on to test the conclusions reached by such argument and discussion by their own experience.

The separating of the arts into aesthetic kinds is not without historic backing. Lessing in his *Laocoön* separates the arts into those of time and space. Music and literature are the arts of time, painting and sculpture those of space. He thinks the distinction important in that different qualities will be required of the practitioners of the two kinds of art. Reynolds takes the same view in his discourses. The artist, he says, has to make his effect "at a blow," while the poet has time to work up his effect. G. E. Lessing praises the sculptural group "Laocoön" in that the sculptor has seized the exact moment to express the agony of the central figure and to give the whole history of the event in its reference to the past and the future.[18] Similarly, Sir Joshua Reynolds reinforces his doctrine that the artist must present the universal as opposed to the

[18] *Laocoön* (1776), trans. W. A. Steel, London, 1930. Pp. 12, 14, 17.

individual, since he has just the one moment to make his effect. Shakespeare may present Julius Caesar in his weaker moments:

. . . 'tis true, this god did shake;
His coward lips did from their colour fly,
And that same eye whose bend doth awe the world
Did lose his lustre . . .

Shakespeare has time to efface this impression and to present Caesar as heroic over-all. The painter, however, who has to produce his effect in one blow, has no such latitude. He must present the hero as heroic, the general as exhibiting the qualities of generalship, and not be led aside by particular features of the individual however intriguing. This kind of distinction, however, is not comparable to the distinction between the higher and the lower senses. Moreover, the distinction is not absolute. Whatever may be said of the painter, our impression of the picture is not *taken* "at a blow." We have to look at it for some time and return to it if we are to get a full impression.

It may be wondered why Hume has been left out in this account of aesthetic experience, when the interest in its subjective side was attributed to him in the beginning. It is a little difficult to "place" Hume in respect to aesthetic theory. He sets himself to give an empirical account of experience, but it is in terms of "facts" that are the products of a very special kind of theory.[19] He speaks always in terms of ideas presented and of accompanying emo-

[19] "Of the Standard of Taste," in *Four Dissertations*, London, 1957. P. 209.

tions or feelings. If a complex phenomenon is to be explained, say, our enjoyment of a painting, it will be in terms of its elements—i.e., simple ideas, together with ideas brought into awareness in accordance with one or another of his laws of association and accompanied by feelings either brought into play directly by the presented ideas or by previous association with the recalled ideas. Hume has a simple theory of human approval—moral and aesthetic. We are pleased by what is beneficial to us and repelled by what is harmful. He now has to explain why art generally should please, and as in his moral theory, he has to invoke the notion of sympathy. We are pleased by scenery or by a picture of scenery that shows a pleasant, smiling landscape, because although we are not directly benefited, say, by a French vineyard, by sympathy with our fellows we feel pleasure at the notion of a prosperous peasantry. Hume has, however, to notice pleasure in a very different kind of landscape. A wild and desolate moor cannot possibly please us by thoughts of its benefit to the human race, but, says Hume, it is one of the "pleasures of imagination." Here, I think that what he has in mind is the wild and lawless which sometimes sweeps us away, as contrasted with the orderly, the neat and complete, which pleases by its conformity to law. To the former we may attribute the sublime, a notion which Hume's fellow thinkers, notably Edmund Burke, found equally intriguing with the beautiful. Having given an account of the beautiful as conforming to the laws of rhythm and harmony, Burke is obliged to find value in another of our experiences, namely, that which by its hugeness, magnificence, even its infinite power or extent, defies all our powers to present it to ourselves as a unity. This defying of the human powers is what constitutes the sublime.[20]

Aesthetic experience has been treated first although interest in it occurred the latest in time. However, the earlier theorists seemed to have been aware of the qualities of aesthetic experience in the sense that they emphasized just those qualities of the objects they valued that we are recognizing as the qualities essential to the arousing of aesthetic experience. One of the most important of these qualities is that which corresponds to distance. I hope to show that distance can be achieved only in relation to an object that is a unity, self-contained, and with no loose ends. It is the loose ends which catch on to elements in our experience and prevent us from maintaining our distance. This may not always be the fault of the artist; it may be something in our experience that forces us to detach one part of the object. Here I will simply say that the requirements for the unity of tragedy set out by Aristotle in the *Poetics* are the qualities enabling the spectators to be spectators.

[20] *A Philosophical Enquiry into the Origin of Our Ideas on the Sublime and Beautiful,* London, 1756.

CHAPTER IV

Structure and Unity
in the Work of Art

It would be true to say, I think, that until the last ten years no one would have thought it anything but a truism to say of a work of art that it must be a unity. The only difference in the past had arisen in the interpretations to be put upon the words and on the degree of strictness with which unity was to be demanded. When Aristotle said that a tragedy must have a beginning, a middle, and an end and gave explicit meaning to these terms, he was not making an extravagant demand but simply making explicit what every reasonable man would take without question.[1] It has remained to our own day to present stories and plays in which it does not seem to be the aim of the author to make clear what is happening and which may be said merely to stop and not come to an end.

Although people of my generation find it natural and fitting to think of a work of art as a unity, we must nevertheless make clear just what is involved in this requirement. Aristotle used the simile of an

[1] *Poetics*, trans. Ingram Bywater, Oxford, 1940. 1450 B26. This edition is used throughout.

organism, and this comparison has persisted.[2] It has
a double aspect, from the point of view of the making of a work of art and of its properties. In fact,
the properties arise from the nature of its making.
We can all see that a flower might cause an artist to
despair, not because it is so beautiful that he would
never be able to make anything to compare with it,
but because it showed plainly that it was formed so
that every one of its features belonged together and
contributed to an end. There are white flowers,
sweet-scented, that open at night, releasing their
scent and glow to attract the moths. There are day-
light flowers with delicate lines leading into their
necks to show the fertilizing insect the way, but
these descriptions show the difficulty of applying
the notion to art, since it is not at all clear that art
has a comparable function. Moreover, there are all
kinds of organisms in nature ranging from the most
delicately small creatures, infinitely varied in their
parts and minutely organized, to the great, almost
amorphous creatures more or less the same all over;
in other words, the range is from flowers and butter-
flies to amoebae and dinosaurs. Aristotle, however, supplies us with a satisfactory way of describing the organic unity of art, though he himself is
concerned chiefly with poetry, and tragedy in particular.

Aristotle did not doubt also that art is imitation,
and at first sight this seems contradictory. To say
that an artist is imitating nature seems to be saying
that he is not creative, but the way in which an

[2] *Poetics*, 1451 A35.

artist imitates nature is threefold. First, he imitates nature in his action of making. Just as nature creates in accordance with the function of what is created, so does the artist. Second, he imitates happenings and things in the product—i.e., he makes things like animals, trees, and men in pictures and statues and plays that are "like" historical events. That is to say, he is acting like nature in creating things of nature. Third, art is imitation from the side of the spectator. The spectator feels as if he were confronted with the real thing (this "as if" must be carefully examined later). This threefold sense of imitation brings out the nature of the unity of the work; just as nature makes organisms, so the artist makes organic unities; consequently the things that he makes are like real things and the spectator is influenced as if he were confronted with real things. Moreover, as Aristotle shows later, art could not do its work on the spectator if it did not possess organic unity and the properties that go with it.[3]

The concept of organic unity is further explicated by Aristotle's dictum that the plot is the soul of tragedy. This is rather an odd notion. Most people tend to think that what matters from an aesthetic point of view is the *manner* of saying things rather than what is said. They do not think of the ability to make plots as the mark of a great writer. It seems to me, however, that Aristotle is right; what marks the great creative writer is the quickening of the imagination by the presented situation or idea that unfolds itself in him and sets him

[3] *Ibid.*, 1450 B26.

to work. It is a great irritation to intellectual people who can write well, but have not this constructive imagination, to see writers producing works of imagination, apparently without effort, that they themselves feel they could do so much better if only they could think of the plots. They think of this "thinking of the plot" almost as if it were a mechanical thing that for some inexplicable reason doesn't happen to them but happens to these inferior writers. C. Day Lewis, the poet laureate, learning that Agatha Christie still had seventeen plots unwritten, is said to have asked her whether she would sell him some of them! He was speaking, of course, in his other persona of "Nicholas Blake." (I do not, of course, wish to deny that non-dramatic poetry is creative—the "soul" here is the vitalizing image which sets creative imagination going.)

To return to the plot as the soul of tragedy, it is that which informs the whole, determining the order of its parts and its size. There is an appropriate size for a mouse and for an elephant, and an appropriate length for a tragedy and a lyric poem. Just as an animal has its infancy, which is leading up to its young manhood and to its end, so a tragedy has a beginning, a middle, and an end. These are not merely temporal terms. The beginning is what leads naturally and inevitably to the central event, the climax, which then relapses into its end.

Perhaps we should say a word about the notion of "soul" in this connection. For Aristotle,[4] "soul" has not the connotation it has for modern thinkers.

[4] *De Anima,* trans. D. W. Hamlyn, New York, 1968. Bk. II, Ch. I, 412 B10, 412 B17.

Soul is that in terms of which the properties of a thing are to be understood, and it is closely connected with the notion of function. Aristotle says that if the eye had a soul it would be that which enabled it to see. The soul of man is that which enables him to function as a human being and therefore most importantly as a citizen. It is manifest in every part of the organism and in every action.

The bearing of this discussion on the nature of art is that if we wish to understand art, we must ask what is its function. The properties of a good knife are connected with the functions of a knife. To say that it has a beautiful handle is to say something about its accidental features. If it is a beautiful *knife,* it is beautiful *as a knife;* that is to say, it has the properties that fit it to cut well. To say of a work of art that it is beautiful is to say that it has the properties that fit it to perform its function.

Here Aristotle, hampered by his place in history, has two approaches. There are the plays of Aeschylus, Sophocles, Aristophanes, and Euripides, all of them highly esteemed by Athenians. Aristotle was not in our position of having the plays of other races and other ages with which to compare his own. For him, tragedy was exemplified by the tragedies of Greece. On the other hand, he had his own idea of what tragedy should accomplish, and for him the two fitted. *These* were the plays displaying the features that tragedy and comedy ought to display in order to fulfill their function in the community, in terms of what they essentially were. For the present we are concerned only with their unity. We shall have to speak later of the effect of art. At the moment we have to notice only that they could not fulfill this effect if they were not unities.

Organic unity has been variously described, but most thinkers would agree that its essential feature is that every part is important to the whole, and that no part can be removed or have another substituted for it without spoiling the whole. This is the kind of assertion that really needs practical testing with pictures, statues, music, poetry, etc. Harold Osborne, rejecting the orthodox view, points out that the better the work of art, the more easily, and with less havoc, can it lose some of its parts.[5] His point is that the greater the work, the more is every part suffused with the quality of the whole, and in support we may note how easy it is to recognize Shakespeare in stray lines, and to appreciate the "Venus de Milo" in spite of its accidental incompleteness.

Before we go any further we must examine more closely the notion of part. In one sense of the word "part," a hand is a part of a human organism; in another sense, a concourse of molecules is a part of a human organism, and in still another, an ounce of flesh is any part. Let us take a simple illustration:

> *Mary had a little lamb,*
> *Its fleece was white as snow;*
> *And everywhere that Mary went,*
> *The lamb was sure to go.*

In one sense, a line is a part of the poem. In the same sense, a word is a part of the line. In a slightly

[5] *Aesthetics and Criticism*, London, 1955. Pp. 240–44.

different sense, a letter is a part of a word, but these are not important senses from the point of view of a poem. Further, if we try to understand the notion of substituting one part for another, we have to find out much more exactly what we are to understand by "substitution." May we equally substitute "Tommy" or "Elsie," or "a girl," or a nonsense word, "exty" for "Mary"? Note that it must be a two-syllable word, and the substitution must be made in every occurrence of the word. Could it be "Mary had a little dog"? If so, it will have to be "coat" and not "fleece," and if it were a little cat, it would have to be "fur." That is to say, "lamb" is not a mere part but an organic part of the verse. In fact, the parts of a poem are not the words but the images, and it is unthinkable that we should change an image without changing or destroying the poem itself.

If it be objected that this is to beg the question and we have so defined "part" that it is an organic part, we may reply that this is the nature of the case and not our own perversity. But surely, it may be argued, there are parts in some less important sense. If I have my head cut off, I am effectively destroyed as a person. If I have my hair cut off, the effectiveness of the destruction will depend on how far I am identified with being long-haired or short-haired. If the cutting off of the hair was the result of a long period of reflection, then it is a different matter from its regular cutting once a month, and if it is just my nails that are cut, the difference is negligible. It is in a purely academic sense that I am different when my nails have been cut. Now it may be argued that there is something in art comparable to the having of my nails cut, but then the point is that if this is so, it is not destructive of an organic unity of the work, since my organic unity has not been destroyed by having my nails cut. The point at issue really is whether a work of art can be essentially damaged by having parts of it removed or replaced, and whether it is *any* parts that are in question, or only "important" parts.

If we take the "Venus de Milo" with its missing arms we do not feel a great sense of the spoiling of the statue; it seems as though the quality of the whole has permeated every part so completely that it is even in the mutilated limbs. Now suppose it had been the head that were missing, the loss would be very much greater; it might even be destructive of the beauty of the whole. Part of the beauty of the statue is the way the head is held on the shoulders, and if neck and head were missing, this might be completely lost.

The same thing is true of substitution of words for one another in poetry. The difficulty here is that if there were a word missing in a manuscript the editors would set to work and confer with one another about which word to put into the blank. If we delete a word for the purpose of experiment I don't quite know how we would read the line; we should have to stop just before, leave a pause, and then go on again: "Bring forth the . . . ; the . . . was brought. In truth it was a noble steed." It is difficult to know just what is being asked of us when this is presented to us as a test. There is not much doubt that we should all of us supply a

word to fill the blank. If we transpose the words—
"Bring forth the steed; the steed was brought. In
truth it was a noble horse"—we can see at once that
this won't do. It depends entirely what kind of substitution is made. If it had been "Bring forth the
mare; the mare was brought. In truth it was a noble
steed," this would not be quite so bad though it
raises irrelevant questions about the sex of the steed.
Perhaps this is not a fair example. What people
have in mind, rather, is that if a poem or painting
is actually presented to us, then if it is a work of
art, its unity will be such that there are no parts
that jar on us. Positively, all the parts belong, and
if we apply ourselves to the understanding of the
work with our critical faculties alert, we shall be
able to see why the parts are as they are, that a
certain line guides the eye back to the center, that
a large mass is counterbalanced by a smaller, more
vividly colored mass on the other side, that a word
expresses just the right feeling for the poem as a
whole, and so on.

The examples used so far have been of small
works; we shall have to say something different
about dramas, long musical compositions, long
poems, and novels. It would not do for a long poem
to be equally "poetical" all through, and there are
certainly some parts of plays that are more easily to
be dispensed with than others. Musical compositions also are sometimes edited for performance and
the resulting piece seems to preserve its unity. This
is not to say that such works are not organic unities, but that some such unities are more minutely
organized than others.

The second feature is that if it is to be an organic unity, a work of art must present an over-all image or character. This is a more difficult notion, though it is very easy to see what it means in a general way. Musical compositions, poems, plays, and paintings all present an impression or a characteristic atmosphere. It is sometimes difficult to track down the source of the impression, but we know what Percy Lubbock means when he calls *War and Peace* "that great shaggy monster."[6] Some works strike us as lucid, brilliant, cold, and clear, while others are warm and intimate. Some strike us almost as cities to be explored and others are façades which present everything on the surface. It is to be supposed that all the parts contribute to this impression just as a human being strikes us as on the whole kindly and tolerant or suspicious and resentful. This general impression is just as difficult to relate to the parts in detail as it is in a work of art.

There is another possible source of the unity of the work of art and that is the intention of the artist. When we were speaking of the condition for organic unity—that no part may be altered or removed without spoiling the whole—we might have thought of cases where the artist himself makes the alteration. Writers and painters vary in the extent to which they alter and correct, and if we are able to look at their notebooks we do not always agree that the alterations are an improvement. When we are considering whether or not an alteration is an

[6] See Chapter 2, note 5.

improvement, it must be in terms of the unity of the work and its general impression that we are approving or disapproving the alteration. If we disagree with the author himself, is he to have the last word? If the author is no longer available and we have no evidence as to his intention, then there is nothing for it but to decide ourselves which, as we say, "fits in better." If the author is able to tell us that he really wants the word we think inferior, then it must be that he has an intention that is not merely to produce a well-organized work.

"Well-organized" is an expression that is not very popular today. It is almost a term of abuse to speak of a play as "well-organized." Certainly no one would claim that the plays in vogue at the moment are organic unities or even meant to be. Good construction is taken to be a mark of insincerity; instead of expressing naturally and uninhibitedly what we are feeling, we have worked on it and dressed it up for public presentation. To old-fashioned people this seems just what should be done to emotion, and it is difficult to see why the actors of the present go to the trouble of hiring halls and presenting themselves on the stage to do what they claim comes naturally to everybody. It is hard to know just what their skill is supposed to lie in and what they have as their object. They must be very altruistic if they are giving up their lives to being play-leaders for adults. It is still more difficult to see why people buy tickets and go to theaters in order to be worked on to provide their own entertainment. The difference is between having a work of art presented to us and being in-

duced to participate in communal "goings on." The
object is supposedly to limber up our emotional behavior, and actors are reformers trying to make it
possible for people to behave less rigidly and get
into touch more easily with their fellows. This may
mean that we have been mistaken about the nature
of art in the past or that art in any recognizable
form is ceasing to exist.

We cannot apply a test based on the standards
by which these new works are to be judged, because their authors would reject the notion of
standards. (One thinks of the Living Theater productions in which the audience is invited to participate and which, in consequence, could not have
any settled plots.) But if they have an object, we
ought to be able to find out whether it is being
achieved or not and state the criteria according to
which a given work is judged as bringing about this
object. If the object is, as they say, to act on people
so that they become more loving and tolerant, then
we ought to be able to compare various works from
this point of view and find out what properties they
have which enable them to bring this end about.
To return to Aristotle, he states clearly what he takes
to be the object of tragedy and sets out the properties of tragedy which enable it to bring about this
end.[7] The end of tragedy, he says, is to arouse pity
and fear in such a way as to purge us of these emotions. He, like the moderns, thinks that tragedy
should have an effect on human beings and their
characters. For him the effect is of calming and tran-

[7] *Poetics*, 1449 B26–28; *Politics*, trans. Benjamin Jowett,
Oxford, 1961, 1341 B37–39.

quilizing our citizens so that after the excitement of
a tragic performance they will go home quietly and
take up their civic duties again. He thinks that we
need to be purged of pity and fear because human beings left alone tend to feel these emotions
to excess and so to become less efficient in their
daily lives. In the *Politics*[8] he speaks of it as the
duty of the ruler to "prescribe" a course of tragic
performances when the populace is overexcited and
apt to cause trouble in the city. The effect of the
tragic performances will be to provide a more suitable object for the emotions, namely, a work of art.
To present *Oedipus Rex* as a tragedy fulfilling the
laws of tragic composition is to present an object
that, while moving the audience to pity and fear,
does it in such a manner that the audience is left
calm and serene, purged of its earlier emotions.
The way in which this is brought about is the way
of organic unity. There are no loose ends, so to
speak; every part of the tragedy is so connected
with every other part that there is nothing to engage
the stray emotions of the audience. A moving event
leads naturally on to the next and the whole is
rounded off with the lowering of the emotional tone.
Aristotle says we ought to prefer probable impos-
sibilities to possible improbabilities, and one reason
for this is that to lead the audience to speculate
about what is unlikely is to arouse an attitude inimical to acceptance.[9]

Perhaps a word should be said as to the meaning
of the word "nature" in which, according to Aris-

[8] *Politics*, Bk. 8, Ch. 7, 1341 B33–1342 A17.
[9] *Poetics*, 1461 B5–7.

totle, art imitates nature. The nature of man is exemplified by Peter, Paul, and John, but what is important is not their individual characteristics, such as being six feet tall, redheaded, or snub-nosed, but in being individuations of the universal man. In the same way, a play is an imitation of the universal action, say, of treachery, not of a particular case of treachery. This is connected with the notion of probable impossibility. A given thing or event is said to be "probable" as an instance of a kind and not in itself. What happens, as a matter of fact, may be highly improbable and as such, not to be imitated in art. If the emotion that is aroused is wonder at a coincidence, this is not the appropriate emotion to be felt toward art. It may be objected here that what is sometimes taken to be the most effective of Greek tragedies, *Oedipus Rex*, is certainly based on a coincidence. The coincidence, however, takes place outside the play and we accept it before we begin. Moreover, the coincidence has been foretold by the oracles and so is not in question. Once the initial improbability has been accepted, everything else follows inevitably.

A modern writer who also takes the view that art presents nature as refined by the creative imagination of the artist is Henry James. In his many accounts of the genesis and growth of his novels he uses the organic metaphor. In his preface to *The Spoils of Poynton,* he used the metaphor of living, growing things with the work of the artist comparable to the gardener's pruning and training. He speaks of the "quickening" of the seed, the germ, the virus, in the fertile soil of the artist's imagination and "the prick of inoculation . . . the whole of the virus being infused by that single touch." Here is James's account of his "taking" of the germ of *The Spoils of Poynton:* "So it was, at any rate, that when my amiable friend, on the Christmas Eve, before the table that glowed safe and fair through the brown London night, spoke of such an odd matter as that a good lady in the North, always well looked on, was at dagger's drawn with her only son, ever hitherto exemplary, over the owner-ship of the valuable furniture of a fine old house just accruing to the young man by his father's death, I instantly became aware, with my 'sense for the subject,' of 'the prick of inoculation.'"[10] Just as for Aristotle, the "imitation" is to be of the universal and not of the actual event all cluttered up with accidentals.[11] James goes on: ". . . when in the next breath I began to hear of action taken on the beau-tiful ground, by our engaged adversaries, tipped each, from that instance, with the light of the high-est distinction, I saw clumsy Life again at her stupid work." Life blurs the clear outlines of the particular case that, in the hands of an artist, has its own logic. There is something to be made of the germ and it is this which the logic of the case both serves and demands; it is an object which will display the germinal situation as self-explanatory and inter-nally consistent and therefore as illuminating, il-lustrating, making vivid, concretizing its appropriate universal or general principle.

If an organic unity has, as its parts, essentials that

---

[10] *The Spoils of Poynton,* London, 1962. Pp. viii, ix.
[11] *Poetics,* 1451 B5–7.

could neither be removed nor transposed without being spoiled and becoming a different object, then it follows that each work of art must be unique. If it were to appear in a different part of space and time it would be the same work of art, and, tautologically, if any part of it were different, it would be a different work of art and probably not a work of art at all. Uniqueness in this sense needs further discussion. We commonly think of human beings as each being unique and it is in this sense that we like to think of works of art as unique also. Miss Ruby Meager raises the possibility of a Bantu knowing basic English, writing in Africa completely by chance and knowing nothing of Browning, producing a complete replica of *Pippa Passes*.[12] This is a possibility only in the logical sense, the sense in which if someone other than Isaac Newton had by chance formulated the theory of gravitation with no grasp of the mathematical implications, he could be said to have discovered the same theorem. (This of course is not relevant to Miss Meager's point.)

In the sense of this example, uniqueness is not impaired. In fact, the example almost confirms our sense of uniqueness. Two people can write the same poem or paint the same picture only in this strained and artificial sense, just as there could be two Sir Winston Churchills in the universe only if we had some kind of theory of history repeating itself and unfolding its pattern over and over again like a roll of wallpaper.

[12] "The Uniqueness of a Work of Art," in *Collected Papers on Aesthetics*, ed. Cyril Barrett, Oxford, 1965.

There is a rather different order of requirements for a work of art. It is sometimes said that a work of art must be original. It is difficult to give a clear meaning to this demand. It is clear, of course, that one artist may not literally copy the work of another unless he makes it clear that this is what he is doing, and insofar as he is literally copying he is not working as an artist at all. Here we must make a distinction. A poet who looks over the shoulder of another poet and writes down word for word what he sees the other write is doing nothing useful for his development as a poet. On the other hand, an artist who sets up his easel beside another artist and copies stroke by stroke what the first one is doing might be learning quite a lot about the technique of painting. The comparable thing for a poet would be to choose a sonnet, for example, from another pen and attempt something in the same manner on the same theme. This brings out an important difference between painting and poetry. In order to create poetry, no manual skill whatsoever is required. If we may speak of the medium at all, it is a medium in a completely different sense from the pigment in painting. For a painter to copy the work of another requires a high degree of manual skill.

Not copying, then, in the literal sense is ruled out as a sufficient requirement of originality as we demand it of an artist. Originality seems more like a directly perceived quality, a freshness and a spontaneity that can be recognized but not inferred. Here again, we can make the contrast between poetry and the plastic arts. If somebody presents us with a poem literally copied from another hand, if the poem has the quality of freshness and originality, then the mere fact that a pretended author hands it to us does not throw doubt on its originality, but if somebody hands us a painting that he has copied from another, then the spontaneity and freshness of the original would not guarantee spontaneity and freshness in the copy. What I have just said will seem to some aestheticians completely without grounds. What, they say, are the marks of this freshness of which you are speaking? I might ask by way of reply, how it is that we recognize youthfulness of appearance? I could not tell anybody the marks by which I recognize youthfulness, but it is plainly to be recognized. It would probably be objected further that I am not satisfied with recognizing freshness, but am going on to claim originality for the work on the ground of its freshness. Certainly I should wish to adduce a laboring style, heaviness, and an artificiality in the choice of words and images as evidence against the originality of the work.

We sometimes feel that it is a mark of originality that we are surprised by the developments of the play or poem, yet we also feel that the end must arise naturally out of the beginning and the middle. These two requirements are not incompatible with one another. It is not a question of seeing in the beginning what is going to happen later on, but after it has happened, recognizing that it was just what we ought to have expected. We have a shock of delight both at seeing how surprising it is and at the same time how inevitable. It is not the logical inevitability of a conclusion of an argument that pleases a mathematician, but its forcefulness. Similarly, aesthetic delight arises naturally from seeing how the end follows inevitably from the earlier events or from the character of the people involved. It is sometimes objected that if surprise is an important element in aesthetic delight, then we can be pleased by it only on our first experience. This is not so; it is not a case of once having had the surprise, we cannot enjoy it as a surprise again. I know some people who have been so delighted with the dénouement that they read a book again and again just in order to savor it. When they get to the last page they are so afraid that their eye will rush on too soon that they cover up the end and force themselves to come to it properly with all that led up to it.

The next requirement seems to have a connection with originality. It is that of sincerity. Some people have even gone so far as to make sincerity a necessary and sufficient condition for excellence in art. Here perhaps I should explain the use of the word "excellence." People who make this claim for the relation between art and sincerity would think of "excellence in art" as a tautology. Works are either art or not. To say of them that they are "excellent" is to add nothing. It would be like taking a measurement very accurately and carefully with the appropriate instrument for our purpose, say, a micrometer in measuring minute parts for machines, a foot rule for measuring the planks for a fence and having made the measurement with all these precautions, to say that is an excellent measurement. It isn't; it's just right. In the same way, if somebody with absolute and utter sincerity and with the minutest exactitude expresses his experience in a given situation then what he has made is exactly right, and "excellent" is not the word to use for it. It is unsuitable from this point of view to compare works with one another and say that one is better than another. They are either just what they should be or they are nothing.

Without going so far as this, however, we might still want to say that a work of art must be sincere if it is to be of any value. It might be objected that we can say *of a man* that he is sincere, and that what we really mean is that the artist must be sincere *as a man* in producing this work if it is to be a work of art. Now of course we have the problem that it might be the purpose of the artist to present views that were not his own, or to present people holding views very different from his own. It might even be that, for some ulterior motive or from an aesthetic point of view, he presented as admirable people whom he really despised. Here we seem to be outside the realm of art altogether and to be treating the making of a work as an action that is either right or wrong. In one sense, of course, it is; we sometimes say of a work that it ought not to have been written. (An example is Lord Moran's medical memoirs of Sir Winston Churchill published immediately after the latter's death.) This is to say nothing about a work's aesthetic worth; it is to treat it entirely as an action coming under moral rules. Benedetto Croce points out that we have to look on the artist in this double sense.[13] We may not dictate to him as an artist what he writes; if, for instance, he feels he must write pornography then he must, but having written it, he then becomes a human being with a duty to his fellows when he chooses whether or not to publish. Artists sometimes blame censors for dictating to them what they shall write or paint; this is not the case at all. They may write and paint what they will; all that somebody with a concern for the welfare of his fellows may say is, "Write what you will, but you must not publish it."

When we speak of sincerity, then, we are sometimes making this moral judgment on the behavior of the artist as a moral being; just as we might say of an ambitious man that he was insincere in his dealings with the powerful, so we might say of an artist that he was insincere in the use he made of his artistic talents. This is not to say anything at all about him as an artist, though of course we might make a moral judgment on a lazy artist that he was wasting his talent as we would on any other kind of artisan or craftsman. If sincerity is to be a word of *aesthetic* praise, then once again it must be an immediately recognized quality as was originality. If sincerity is to be a quality of any kind other than this immediately recognizable one, it will require the presence of two states that we can compare with one another. For instance, if we say of a man that he is insincere in what he says to somebody, we must know what he says of this person when he

[13] *Aesthetics,* trans. Douglas Ainslie, 1953. See articles on aesthetics in *Encyclopaedia Britannica,* 14th ed., 1929.

is not present; we must be able to say that he thinks one thing and says another. Now this is what we cannot do in the case of art. We haven't got one set of works showing the real feelings and opinions of the artist with which we can compare what he is saying in the work which we are criticizing as insincere. What we *have* got are facts about his life, his conduct, and the principles by which he lives, which sometimes seem to be completely inconsistent with the principles that he seems to approve in his work.

However this may be, criticism along these lines is not criticism of the work but of the man's conduct. Patent insincerity in the work could present itself only as inconsistency within the work. There is a very mild example of this kind in *Cranford*. Mary Smith, the storyteller, is an unsophisticated young girl, and when she is describing a dinner party given by one of the old ladies of Cranford, she records their habit of pouring all the wine that is left into one bottle and corking it with brown paper. She adds, "Captain Brown though a military man does not seem to have enjoyed wine much, I noticed he always refused it at these dinner parties." That would be all right, but a little later Mary is advising Miss Matty, when she is to entertain a male cousin, to throw away the wine and start a new bottle. Which is the real Mary Smith? The one who wondered why Captain Brown, though a military gentleman, would not take wine or the one who knew very well what was wrong with it?

The notions of freshness, sincerity, and originality are interconnected in such a way that people seem to become confused and think that skill, experience, and training destroy these properties. A film producer is at this time in England looking for eight young girls with no experience in acting to portray the very short passage in their lives when they cease to be little girls and become adult. British Actors' Equity is objecting that he has not even considered any of its experienced film actresses, but he maintains that to have acted is to disqualify them from portraying immaturity and lack of sophistication. Why should this be? If a young person with dramatic skill can portray a person of experience, why may not a person of experience portray an unsophisticated young girl? There seems to be some question of sincerity involved. It is somehow held to be insincere if a person of experience "pretends" to be innocent, but not if an innocent person "pretends" to be sophisticated. There is a paradox of naïveté—as soon as one becomes aware of being naïve the quality disappears, although Le Douanier Rousseau wrote to a friend, "If I have kept my naïveté, it is because M. Gérôme, who was professor at the École des Beaux-Arts and M. Clément, Director of the École des Beaux-Arts, Lyon, always told me to keep it."[14] Is this an example of present or past naïveté?

I imagine that if we could induce the moderns to speak in general terms or to listen to us while we so spoke, they would at least agree with the necessity for sincerity in art. I take their insistence on doing one's "own thing," on not producing

[14] Letter written to André Dupont, art critic, Paris, 1910.

work from scripts or from instructions, to be based on their desire that what they do should come out red hot from their emotions uncontaminated by any kind of thought about what impression they are making or what other people think about them. If their work had to go through the intellect I imagine that they would be afraid it would be spoiled *en route.* I do not agree that this freedom from thought guarantees sincerity; it is not only in the intellect that we desire to conform. If we are acting entirely emotionally, there will be a desire to do and feel the kinds of things that our fellows are doing and feeling. The main difference lies in the kind of people *with* whom young actors and actresses, painters and writers want to feel. They have no use for experts in any sense of the word. The expert is the one who would impose standards on them in the interest of what they would take to be an abstract view of art.

My own view is that the only safeguard for making sure we really feel our own feelings is to hang on to the appropriateness of the object of feeling. The late Dr. C. E. M. Joad traced the source of what he called "modern decadence" to the "disappearance of the object."[15] There are the modern "mystics" who praise the virtues of contemplation and explore all sorts of ways of throwing themselves into this state, but for the sake of being in the state and not for its true purpose, which is to become aware of an object worthy of contemplation. It is one thing to follow the great mystics of religion in

[15] *Decadence,* London, 1948. Ch. 10.

their instructions for becoming aware of the presence of God; it is quite another thing to take mescaline in order to enjoy the state of contemplation. Similarly, to investigate ways of throwing ourselves into a state of aesthetic contemplation for its own sake is equally unrewarding. There is only one way of achieving the aesthetic state and that is to become acquainted with and study the great art objects of the world.

Whatever theorists may say as to the importance of the unity of a work of art, practical critics assume it in their evaluations of works. There are devices regularly used by poets, composers, and painters that result in organic unity in the sense that they facilitate the taking in of the object in a single perception and present it for further study. Recurrence, that is, the reappearance of an element, is one of these devices. A theme is repeated in a musical composition, a chorus in a poem or a song, form in buildings. Rhyme is the simplest way in which recurrence is used in poetry, and this shows us that we cannot speak literally of a recurrence of the same element. Just as two words with different meanings may rhyme, so a theme taken up by a different instrument in an orchestral piece cannot be said literally to be the same theme.

Rhythm is another device to bring about unity—the beat of stress and unstress is the same throughout a poem, as is the tempo in music, though there can be variations for special effects. In painting and sculpture the place of rhythm is taken by the emphasizing of some parts in relation to others. It may be that the dominating element is in the center of

the work, and there will be devices of perspective
and lighting which lead the eye to the important object. Symmetry may be used of both the visual and
auditory arts. It applies to the balancing of masses
against each other in a painting, and in the literary arts by the treating of similar themes side by
side. King Lear and his daughters are "balanced" by
a similar set, Gloucester and his sons. The most
important, though, of the devices for achieving
unity is the development of a plot in literature,
and the development of a theme in musical compositions.

If we revert to our account of aesthetic experience, it will be seen that these devices may all
be looked upon as enhancing the ease, and therefore the pleasantness, of aesthetic appreciation. Not
only is a picture framed so that our eye is not
tempted beyond its borders, but also the lines are
so disposed as to direct the eye back again and
along such lines as to yield harmonious movement
of the perceiving organ. The placing of emphasis
on parts of the work tells us what to look for, so
that we are not lost in a bewildering medley of
separate parts. The formal arrangement of a work
guides the eye or the ear, tells us when we may
relax, in short, tells us how we must take the
object.

CHAPTER V

Art and the Community

So far we have been concerned with the meaning of "work of art," first in the sense of its denotation—i.e., the objects to which the term is suitably applied; second, with the experience appropriately aroused by these objects; and third with the characteristic of the work that seems to be correlated most closely with the demands of the experience, namely, its unity. It now remains to discuss it from the point of view of the society in which the artist works and, finally, from the point of view of what the artist himself conceives himself to be doing. In this chapter we shall be concerned largely with the place of art and the artist in society.

One of the most surprising features in the history of art criticism is the hold that the theory of art as imitation maintains on the expert and ordinary viewer alike. Plato and Aristotle did not feel that they had to justify this view of art, but simply accepted it and discussed its nature and implications. It has lasted with varying degrees of intensity to the present time. One of the chief criticisms of modern art by the man in the street is that he does

not know what it is meant to be. The theory of imitation has been held in extreme form by the most
surprising people, notably by Leonardo da Vinci,
who committed himself to the most unscientific
statements about the effect of paintings on men
and animals.[1] It is true that he was putting forward the claims of painting and sculpture to be
considered as "fine arts" along with poetry, rather
than as crafts, so that he was probably speaking
more loosely than was his custom. Even so, it is
surprising to find statements like the following:
"I once saw a dog, deceived by a portrait of his
master, giving him a joyful welcome; and I have
observed dogs trying to bite dogs represented in
a painting." He also claimed to have seen monkeys
playing with paintings of monkeys. This is difficult
to believe, and it is also difficult to understand why
he should have committed himself to such statements. He is on slightly less questionable grounds
when he speaks theoretically. He says that painters
lead people to worship the Deity in their work, a
result which poets could never achieve. Similarly,
he says people have been known to fall in love with
a person presented in a painting, but never with the
object of a love poem. Poets can present their objects only a piece at a time, but painters present
us with absolute, out and out, unadulterated imitation, making people and even animals behave in
the presence of the painting as if it were the real
thing.

[1] "Paragone," from *Trattato della Pittura*, trans. Irma A.
Richter, Oxford, 1949.

On the other hand, Leonardo presumably in his more "professional" moments[2] speaks quite differently of painting when he calls it an experimental method of pursuing knowledge and expressing it. The man who wishes to understand the world as spatial and space as an abstraction—that is, as it is in itself—turns to Euclid. He who wishes to understand the world of objects, not as it appears as one might think, but *as it is* for perception, turns to painting, and there is a science of painting just as exact as Euclid's geometry. This science includes an understanding of all the methods of presenting depth, variations in depth, and relative positions by means of shading, variation in color and in size. These are not devices, as one might think, for presenting the *illusion* of depth. They are ways of making clear what depth is in itself from a given point of view.

Must we at this point give up altogether the notion of art as imitation? Like many of the concepts of aesthetic theory, imitation turns around in one's hands as one examines it, and it will be shown that imitation is to be interpreted as of reality and not of appearances. In this connection, it is instructive to compare the statuary of classical Greece with that of India. The Indian statues make no attempt to relate the inner and outer structure of the human frame. The neck is a cylinder set firmly on the shoulders with no attempt to suggest the bony structure. The Hindu sculptors were developing a system of conventions for presenting the human

[2] *Loc. cit.*

form not as a realistic imitation but for their own purposes.

In contrast, one has only to compare the earlier with the later examples of Greek sculpture to see that the artists were pursuing the means of presenting the human form as a highly organized structure and not as a surface. They were developing conventions for presenting the human frame in all its complexity, and we may see the ambiguity of "imitation" when we recall that Plato strongly objected to realistic developments both in art and poetry. He thought of these developments as making art more imitative and therefore worse. To simulate the real was for him simply to duplicate appearances, a thing that any one of us can do by taking a mirror and twisting it around to take in the world of surrounding objects.

Aristotle did not object to the increasing realism of the imitations of artists and poets, and here the fundamental difference between his views and those of Plato becomes evident. It lies both in their view of the nature of art and of the effects of art on the human character. Though both accept without question that art is imitation, for Plato imitation is essentially of appearances, for Aristotle, of the truly real.

Here we may go on to our next point in which lies the chief difficulty in accepting the view of art as imitation. If art is imitation, why is it worth doing? Plato consistently answered that it is not worth doing. There are a few useful functions we may ask of the artists. We need them to build temples to the gods and to adorn them with statues and friezes in honor of the gods and heroes. We need them to write odes in honor of the great occasions in the life of the city when our heroes return from war or in festivals of worship of the gods, and for these purposes, stylized unrealistic works are more effective. Apart from this, artists and their work are a bad influence in the community. But it is only if art is imitation of *appearances* that we need reach this conclusion. Leonardo takes a middle course by insisting that imitation is of what things really are from a given point of view.

There is one problem that Plato does not mention, though I cannot help feeling that it must have been one of the most important factors in his dislike of the presence of artists in the city. The work of everybody else can be regulated. At any given time the shoemakers are making shoes, the tailors are making clothes, the soldiers are practicing their defensive skill, the rulers are deliberating or pursuing the studies that make them fit to be rulers. If there are any artists, there is no place where they ought to be at a given time, no particular work they ought to be doing. They would arouse discontent among the workers who saw them strolling around the city during normal working hours. An artist, as Plato knew,[3] is wayward and erratic in his habits and even, in moments of inspiration, in a divine frenzy. We have to choose—we must either suffer the artists to go their own disorderly uncitizenlike way and enjoy the results, or we

[3] *Ion,* trans. W. R. M. Lamb, London, 1927. Pp. 534–35.

must regulate the artist and put up with the quiet, orderly citizens who consequently make to order odes to the heroes and statues in their honor. Even here, we have a problem. There will not be very many occasions for civil celebration, and how are our artist-citizens to learn their craft?

Aristotle definitely thought of art as the imitation of the ideal which is also the real. As such, it had its use in presenting men with things as they ought to be. It increases our knowledge of things and people as they really are, and exercises us in the appropriate emotional reaction to such objects. This moving between the notion of things as they ought to be, and as they are, needs explanation.

Aristotle really accepts the equivalence. A rose *as it actually is* in the garden is a more or less imperfect copy of the real thing. If someone were to ask a gardener what a rose was, he would not reply that it is a cankered, one-sided bloom that is brownish at the edge of its petals. This, unfortunately, is what this rose *actually* is, and it is a falling short of the real thing—the rose which has "five petals, obcordate, the length of the calyx, inserted into the neck of the calyx . . . ," to quote from a *Gardeners' Dictionary* of 1807. More recent gardening books do not find it necessary to give descriptions of roses, so sure are they that we know *what a rose ought to be*, even though what we actually meet is something far different. In this connection, we may recall Oliver Cromwell's pseudo-modest demand to be painted "warts and all."

In many other times and places, imitation has been held to have important functions. In primitive

communities the essential magical rites for the regu-
lating of the crops were by imitation. The realistic
drawings of animals on the walls of caves are
thought to have had the partly magical function of
inducing nature to produce more and more things
like this and the sheerly practical function of training a hunter's eye so that he would know just where
to thrust his spear. In Ancient Egypt the faces on
the mummy cases had the practical function of
guiding the soul back to its own body. In our own
day, they have the function of reminding us of
people and places. Even here there is an echo of
Aristotle's insistence that what is to be imitated
is the ideal and not the actual. The people who
know about boats, fishermen and sailors, are apt
to look very closely at a picture of a boat and
criticize it on the grounds that the boat would cap-
size at the slightest breeze. Riders and drivers of
horses are equally critical of knock-kneed, broken-
winded specimens. Some people might look on this
as irrelevant criticism, thinking that it does not matter whether the boat would be able to last in a
tempest or not, just so long as it is a patch of color
or a mass needed at that particular space in the
composition.

This point of view is harder to maintain in the
case of the literary arts. In Pope's satirical description,

So well-bred spaniels civilly delight
In mumbling of the game they dare not bite,

the truth of the observation of the spaniel's habits
matters; it would not do if it were not true that a

spaniel is trained to bring back the game un-broken.[4] That is to say, we want the true nature of the object respected. In the picture we want the true nature of the boat or of the horse respected. Here, however, we may raise our own objections. It might be that the artist needed a cockleshell and not a proper boat, or a broken-down horse rather than a "steed." Here we are on a slippery slope because at once we begin to think he will then be portraying the true nature of a faulty boat or of an imperfect horse and there is no knowing where this process would stop.

There is another important use for imitative art. There are illustrated books of flowers and birds, maps and charts, cookery books. This use of art is now almost extinct because of the growth of me-chanical processes—photography, films, and so on. If we were to look back at books of an earlier age and notice the loving care with which a plant was presented in a botany book, showing all its parts in the most minute detail, we might almost think of beauty as a by-product of such loving care in a practical work. Certainly there is little that is more beautiful than the illuminated manuscripts of the Middle Ages, with the minute care to preserve the text and to show the appropriate natural objects brought into mind by the text.

We now come to what we may call provisionally a "use of art," namely entertainment. The phrase "the use of art" is controversial because many peo-ple would deny that anything that may be used is

[4] See J. R. K. Elliott, "Poetry and Truth," in *Analysis*, Vol. 27, No. 3.

rightly to be called "art" and, vice versa, deny that
art is rightly to be called "entertainment." On the
other hand, we may claim that entertainment is an
important social activity, and that if it is to be done
it should be done well. There is an ambiguity here.
We might say that if burglary is to be done, it
should be done well, that is to say, the burglar
should get away with a big haul so cleverly that he
is never detected. On the other hand, to be a burglar at all is not to *do* well, and we might say that
it would be a good thing if burglars were inefficient.
However, I myself would prefer to be burgled by
a professional. The amateur tends to panic and to
hit people on the head in a frenzy of apprehension.
This is to assume that burglars are not sadists and
would prefer to go quietly about their work and
withdraw.

We have to decide here into which category en-
tertaining falls. Are critics saying that people ought
not to be entertained, or that they ought not to be
entertained by what in another context is art? In
other words, is the question one of the worthy em-
ployment of our spare time or of keeping art from
trivialization? The first question is really a consideration of social philosophy and not properly of
aesthetics. Only the strictest of puritans would
maintain seriously that people ought not to wish to
be entertained and that they should spend their
time either in working or resting in order to work
better. From an aesthetic point of view, the second
question is the important one. According to this,
people ought not to go to theaters simply to pass a
pleasant three hours or to expect entertainment to

be put on with this sole purpose. This is a difficult question to settle. We might hold the view that there is such a thing as light art, that we do not always feel equal to a really serious art experience, but that we feel the need for watching something or listening to something that takes less concentrated effort. It would be too emotionally exacting to see tragedies frequently. I imagine that mathematicians sometimes indulge themselves with light problems, crossword puzzles, or with playing the more or less intellectual games.

Let us pursue the notion of "light art." There are of course comic operas, farces, and revues as opposed to grand opera, comedies, and tragedies. I am anxious here not to be misunderstood. I put comedies and tragedies together on the serious side because I think that comedy is just as serious as tragedy, and of no less aesthetic importance. I am contrasting both with something less ambitious, with a work that is not intended to call the serious powers of the intellect into play. We now come on to two separate but related notions—the notion of being of a good kind and of being good of its kind. It would not be possible, I think, to say that farces and revues were necessarily of the inferior kind, nor even that it would be easier to please with a farce that was not good of its kind than with a serious work that also was not good of its kind. Being "good of its kind" seems to be an essential to pleasing in any way, but a farce that was good of its kind would please differently from a serious work that was good of its kind. We may note here, too, that there are good "bad books," i.e., good of their kind, and bad "good books," i.e., of a good kind, but not succeeding. "Bad books" are those that do not, so to speak, enter themselves for the aesthetic stakes—their authors do not ask for review copies to be sent to the *Times Literary Supplement*—they put themselves forward as honest entertainment. *Gone With the Wind* belongs to this category, as well as the novels of Marie Corelli—*The Sorrows of Satan*, etc. Bad "good books" have aimed but failed to reach the standard of "novels." Examples of bad "good books" are not hard to find, though dangerous to mention! This *is* a judgment which is a matter of taste and anyone's examples will probably be rejected by someone else. I suggest *The Fountain* by Charles Morgan, *Dr. Zhivago* by Boris Pasternak, *Lolita* by Vladimir Nabokov, *The Forsyte Saga* by John Galsworthy. *Lorna Doone* has been suggested by some critics to figure in such a list; my only doubt would be whether it ought to appear in any list of good books, bad or good. The comparison is between horses run by their owners quite contentedly at second-class race courses and a Derby failure. I hesitate to judge between the two.

There is a similar distinction to be made between art, literature, and music that is pleasing at certain ages but ceases to please when the listener becomes mature. Even here, the distinction is not as simple as it seems; there are good children's books and bad children's books, there is music and poetry that are seen by people of sensibility to be rightly enjoyed by the young, though not by themselves. There is also work seen to be rightly enjoyed by the young and still enjoyed by people of mature

sensibility. It is not necessary that work should be
seen to be pleasing at all ages in order for it to be
pronounced good. Keats is essentially a poet for
the young, and older people can perceive his charm
even though they cease to feel it. On the other
hand, there are some works, especially musical, that
in later years we are ashamed of having enjoyed.
Perhaps "ashamed" is the wrong word. We might
say rather that we recognize that in enjoying that
particular work we were displaying bad taste. (A
musically gifted acquaintance of mine claims that
the Beatles' music is excellent for five minutes—
Bach's for eternity.)

I imagine that our chief criticism of "entertainment art" is that its makers almost necessarily have
a double standard, the excellence of the art itself
and its excellence as entertainment. We might
compare sport from this point of view. The excellence of club football is sometimes sacrificed to the
necessity of winning at all costs. Plato speaks about
the activities of politicians in a democratic community in much this way.[5] A statesman carrying on
his own activity well may really have the interest
of the community at heart, but in a democratic
community he has got to induce people to entrust
him with the task that he feels well adapted to perform. Here is the snag. In order to be allowed to
perform his own activity, he has to become skilled
in quite a different kind of performance, namely,
the pleasing of the electorate. This is true of any
kind of activity that depends on popular support.

[5] *Republic,* trans. J. L. Davies and D. J. Vaughan, Cambridge, 1886. Bks. 8, 9.

Doctors do not need to present themselves to us and appeal to be allowed to look after our health; they simply become good doctors. The statesman is not allowed simply to be a good statesman, he has to be a good popular performer before he can begin. Now if art is to be allowed to be entertainment in an important sense, then playwrights, novelists, composers, and instrumentalists have to consider the two things—they have to prevail on us to allow them to do their job, and then actually do their job. This, I think, is at the root of the dislike of the notion of art as entertainment. There is the picture in the mind of the serious patron of the arts of mindless people diverting the talent and industry of artists into the trivial field of catering to their desire for light entertainment.

This picture is misleading in a way. There can also be a pretense at seriousness, which is almost worse. Tolstoy sketched a similar picture of audiences' persuading themselves of their great sensibility and sympathy with human suffering because they found themselves moved by the fate of imagined beings in play and opera.[6] It is easy to indulge in sympathy if it is not to lead to any action for the relief of real suffering, and Czarist Russia was not noted for its sympathy with suffering. At this point we can see that Tolstoy's notion of serious art is rather different from the one assumed in the preceding paragraphs. For Tolstoy, serious art is art that prevents this easy assumption of sensibility and by its simplicity increases brotherly love among

[6] *What Is Art?* trans. Aylmer Maude, London, 1930. Pp. 274 ff.

human beings. So-called "serious art" divides people into those who are able to appreciate it and
those who cannot. One needs to cultivate enjoyment of "great" art, music, and literature, while
simple peasant songs, dances, and music can be
enjoyed by anybody. In keeping with this view,
Tolstoy refuses to admit that the "great works" of
the world are art at all. They are merely masquer-
ading as art.

The conclusion to be drawn, if any, is that if people want to go to the theater and to concerts and if
there are others who are willing to write the kinds
of things they want to see and hear, then it is a
good thing that there should be critics who see
that what is given to them is "good of its kind."
We cannot legislate about the kind of thing that
people are to be allowed to see, but only to insist,
as far as we are able, that it should be good of its
kind.

A further use of art in the community is the great
enlarging of experience to be obtained through
reading and listening to music and plays. We are
so steeped in the literature of the Bible and of
Shakespeare, for example, that it is hard for us to
imagine what our inner state would be like if we
were confined to our own personal experience. People may be happily married, but their experience is
immensely enlarged by having lived in the context
of a larger world that includes Abraham and Sarah,
Darby and Joan if we are to be allowed to include
folk tale; people may be thwarted in love, but if
each is simply suffering his own experience without
Romeo and Juliet, or Jacob laboring fourteen years

to win Rachel, he has no means of universalizing his own suffering or even of seeing it as it is. Perhaps a word should be said as to the usefulness of recognizing that one's own state is general. It is not quite like having an illness diagnosed, though there is a similarity. Suppose one were confronted for the first time with painful swellings, spots, fever, loss of appetite, and there were no doctors or knowledgeable relatives to say "measles." There is no magical efficacy in the word "measles," but there is the reassurance that it is a recognized condition and that it is therefore manageable. Someone knows how to cope with it. Similarly, if, sunk in despair, one comes upon a presentation of one's predicament in a striking and moving dramatic form, one feels that here is something recognizable and universal and therefore to be coped with or, at least, to be borne.

There are differences of opinion as to whether the value of art lies nearer to the category of knowledge or nearer the category of feeling. It may be that it belongs to both categories in that it makes it possible to *know* feeling rather than simply to suffer it. Charles Williams in *War in Heaven* points out that in the events of our own life we are submerged in our practical preoccupations and therefore unable to experience emotion in its pure form, and certainly not to see it as it is. A man may be overwhelmed with misery when his wife is on the point of dying, but is unable simply to feel his sorrow because practical worries flood in—how will he be able to look after the children, will he have to send them away?—while all the time he is really wishing to feel simple sorrow. Our only chance of "knowing" the emotions in their pure form is in literature and the arts generally.

Moreover, in real life we never see anything through to a conclusion, everything is left with loose ends leading on and on indefinitely and in varying directions. It may be that some people would think of this as a very good reason for condemning art; in presenting us with well-organized unities, with well-rounded-off plays, artists are misleading us. My contention is that there is nothing misleading here at all. Nobody is led to think that this is what life is actually like; they are simply given a more complete view of the things that they know vaguely and incompletely. If somebody objects that this is not knowledge in the proper sense of the word—that is to say, we are not being given knowledge in the sense that the thing we know is put under its right heading, assigned to its category —this is true. What we are being given is something much more important, knowledge by complete and minute acquaintance.

When one thinks of art as being "used," art therapy immediately springs to mind. This brings out the ambiguity of the word "using." Therapists do not *use* art, they use what we know of the making of art to help those who are so badly inhibited that they are unable to take their place in normal living. The theory is that expression in words or movement, sometimes with paintbrush in one's hands, is natural to us all, but that many of us are incapable of performing this natural function. This is not to use art in the bad sense of making it subsidiary to

something else. It is to use something that happens
naturally and to direct it toward a good end. We
may compare the way in which a community uses
mother love to get its children looked after well.
The connection with art considered as the producing of valuable objects is incidental. Art, like the
things made by children and by the mentally re-
tarded, is a release of activity, but what is released
has to be judged by the ordinary criteria of art.
Some non-artists are set free as artists are set free,
but their work is not of equal value. Creative
imagination is not a flowing or a pouring out of inhibited material, it is constructive work upon the
material so released.

Imagination is often wrongly conceived. If somebody says, "Suppose there were an abyss outside
the door, and if we were to open it we would be
upon the edge of nothingness," he is supposed to
be imaginative; but this process is not to be compared with the act by which we maintain our whole
world as a unity. The abyss would be all very well
if it were the beginning of a new construction, such
as H. G. Wells might have given us. It is not idly
that we speak of Tolstoy or Shakespeare as creating their world; they create not only a spatiotemporal world, but a world of characters that present
themselves much more powerfully to the imagination than the world of historical characters.

This process of creating a world may be compared with the feat we all perform when we accept
the small part of the world we know as a part of a
unity that spreads out spatially to the Arctic re-
gions in one direction, through Europe and Africa

to the Antarctic in another, and through China around to the Americas and back. But not only this —it spreads out to include an infinitely expanding universe, reaching back in time before history began and forward into the unknown future. We perform this feat in a small way and with the help of the creative artist when we find ourselves, halfway through a description, suddenly finding that we have got to change our construction. We are suddenly told that our hero turns to the right down Chancery Lane and find that we had constructed the scene the other way around and have to begin again. This is a feat of imagination that we are performing all the time, and much more remarkable than any idle fancying such as supposing that there were an abyss outside the door.

The digression upon imagination was for the purpose of bringing out the difference between the artist and the non-artist. Constructive imagination of our *own* world is common to us all, though there may be some mental illnesses in which this faculty is impaired. The flowing out of a number of associated images is also common to us all, except for the inhibited, and it is this that can be stimulated by art therapy. A very few of us can so organize the flow of images that it makes a world—these are the artists.

We now come to a much more acceptable "use" of art. Before we were laying ourselves open to the objection that art by its very definition must not be used. It is valuable in itself and for its own sake, and we are sinning against its very nature to think of "using" it in any kind of way. Architects occupy a very special position in our world in that they are literally creating our environment. When we think of our enjoyment of our natural landscape, we are not thinking in terms of art at all, but in terms of what is simply given. Architects have to study this given and modify it, even enhance it, and at the same time make useful constructions in which people may live and carry on their various activities. Factories, schools, housing estates, offices, shops, and theaters all have to be fitted into an already existing environment with its own character. Citizens who do not very much like the constructions of modern architects are apt to demand of them that they should make their buildings as unnoticeable as possible. They think of the architect as somebody whose duty it is to provide us with the buildings we need without spoiling what we have become used to. This is far from the way in which the architect thinks of his work. He alone among artists is hampered by having to adapt his creations to an environment that already has its own character. He can never begin with a blank canvas. In a few cases he may be able to plan a new town, and here the already established environment would be not so much a hindrance as a challenge. He would adapt his new city to a situation on a plain or in the hills, with woods around or with an open space. This is almost like the challenge that the sonnet form presents to a poet or the sonata form to a composer. The chief difference here is that the architect has the extra problem of adapting what he is to make to the life of the community. I know little of the limitations placed upon the architect by civil councils in England employing his services, but here I must say I think the architect fails. It may be that he is following instructions, but in the housing estates there seems to have been very little thought given to the quality of the life that will be led by its inhabitants. There are rows upon rows of houses, with no center to the community where the housewives will meet for their shopping, no "local" where the men will come together for a drink in the evening, nor a place for the young people on the weekend. If they are to go anywhere, it will be from the bus station to a neighboring town.

Another depressing feature is that very often the neighboring town has been "developed," and anyone arriving there unexpectedly would not be able to tell whether it was a West Country, a South Coast, or a Northern town. There will be a Sainsbury's, a Marks & Spencer's, a Woolworth's, etc., with the same windows and the same packaged goods on display. There is no particular reason for going to any one place rather than another or any one part of it rather than another. This is not the fault of architects—they are working in the present age and environment. They are in the ungrateful position of having to create the conditions of the new life that many of us "want" to live in the practical sense but that makes no strong appeal to the life of imagination, which tends to dwell in the past. Our churches are an illustration of this duality of everyday life contrasted with the imagined life. We think of country churches with their heritage of stained-glass windows, tombs, and inscriptions as a record of the past—the ringing of the bells as we walk along the field paths, the open doors on a sunny Sunday morning with psalm and anthem pealing out; we would resist the destruction of the churches, *but we do not go in and pray and sing.*

This is the background in which present day architects produce the buildings that are suited to our ways of living, but not to the life of our country in literature, which is still powerful in the imagination. It may be that I am writing too much from the point of view of the declining generation, but I think my experience is typical of many. I go down to High Street not with a conscious thought of the past, but feeling as if I were going to the village of my childhood. Each time, there is a new shock as I see the new square flat buildings in place of the row of little shops, each with its own character—the butcher's with its wrought iron railings and two trees, the King's Arms with its perilous steps, and the old post office with its bow windows. These are the things that stay with one.

Architecture is in a special position, too, from the point of view of its insistence on our notice. We need not go to galleries or to theaters or concert halls, but we must see our buildings. Even if we do not look at them, they color our whole lives. People walking or riding past them in buses to work every morning are depressed or exhilarated by what is there. People think that country folk do not appreciate their surroundings because they do not go to the scenic spots as do tourists. It is enough for them that the beauty is there. To work in a room "with a view," is to work contentedly—we

know it is there, even though we do not continually
look at it. It is depressing to work with a window
looking out on a blank wall, even when we are not
looking at it.

Speaking entirely as an amateur, I feel that architects have another handicap. When our churches
and cathedrals were designed and built, there was
a very definite community life of which they
formed the center. It is difficult to think of a "center" of community life now, though it is noteworthy
that our best new buildings are concert halls,
theaters, and even cathedrals that manage to keep
their life going by serving a very large area. Offices,
factories, and dwelling places have no functional
life of their own, since their construction is a du-
plication of cells rather than an organization of
varying activities. A block of little boxes each with
a family in it or with a desk, a director, and a sec-
retary does not lend itself to a pleasing overall design. People tell us of community halls in blocks of
flats, but it is no use to give facilities for an activity
that has not already declared itself. If it does not
naturally belong to the life being lived there, it will
not be used. There is one center of communal life
that is entirely new and has come into being of
necessity. In England launderettes on a Sunday
morning are filled with men, each with a car outside and his family wash, and they chat together,
I am sure, rejoicing in their freedom from the pa-
rental tyranny they suffered in their youth, of Sunday school, church, and choir!

Modern conditions further yield both a handicap
and an advantage to architects. With very few ex-

ceptions medieval builders of churches and cathedrals did not have to tear down beloved buildings
or obstruct views to get a location for their constructions; today architects are unjustly felt to be
responsible for the replacing of, say, the pleasant,
harmonious houses of a Bloomsbury Square, by the
uniform, flat, square buildings of the University of
London. Architects are essentially connected with
"town and country planning," but the inevitable
destruction is "planned" before the architect is
called in. The compensating advantage of modern
inventiveness lies in the wealth of new material to
challenge the man who is to use concrete, prefabri-
cated blocks, etc.

Architecture is unique in another respect. In the
works of the other arts we can ask, however
vaguely, what they are about. This is true even of
music, but architecture is not about anything at all.
Churches are *for*, not *about*, the worship of God,
though buildings may represent our view of the
relationship of God to his people. Europeans speak
of churches as reaching up into the sky and feel
that this represents human aspirations toward God,
but a Moslem of my acquaintance rejects this description as typical of religious feeling. He thinks
of the domes of the mosques as the gathering together and the sheltering of the worshipers by their
God. This aspect of architecture, i.e., as presenting
an attitude rather than its object, led Hegel to speak
of architecture as "symbolic." He was not putting
forward a general theory of art as symbolic, as
some modern thinkers do, but distinguishing as
symbolic a historical phase in the development of

art. Primitive art is symbolic in the sense that the general notions of the universe achieved by primitive people are vague, amorphous, and generally unsuited for artistic expression. Hegel describes the grotesque sculptures of Egypt and India as belonging notably to this phase. Still more revealingly, architecture is seen as the typical art.[7] To make a temple in which God's people may be gathered together, it is not necessary to have thought deeply about the nature of God; we are simply making a place in which we may worship an unknown but omnipotent Being.

The second phase in the development of art is the classical period of which sculpture is the typical art. In classical Greece, philosophers had thought clearly about the nature of the gods and men, but they had not uncovered the disturbing mass of material that constitutes modern knowledge of human beings. Philosophical ideas were then exactly suited for clear presentation. For once in the history of the world the content was exactly fitted to the form, and, as G. W. F. Hegel says, beauty was achieved in a clear and unequivocal sense. The romantic period has poetry as its typical art, and here too much is known and in too great detail for adequate expression. Once again we may say many things about art—it is interesting, evocative, perceptive, etc.—but not that it is sheerly beautiful. We might say of romantic art that it is emotionally appealing, and of symbolic art that it is sublime, but only of classical art that it is unequivocally

[7] *The Philosophy of Fine Art*, London, 1920. Vol. 1, pp. 103–22.

beautiful. Appreciation of the beauty of nature passes through these same phases, naturally enough since for Hegel nature is constituted by our perception of it, though not quite as is art. Hegel's description of the contrast is that nature has passed through the mind once, art twice. This makes the beauty of art superior to the beauty of nature.

Symbolism as a general theory of art is valuable chiefly as an answer to the question as to the status of works of art in the universe. Some things are easy to place—living things belong to the world in their own right—some things are made for use, but we then have the category of things that are made for some other reason. Much time and thought has been spent in trying to determine this reason.

Imagine a savage looking around a modern room; plants in pots and fish swimming about in tanks would not worry him, though he might wonder why anybody thought it worthwhile to bring these things under cover. Tables and chairs he could make sense of, though he might think that a table turned upside down would make a splendid canoe. A looking glass on the wall, however, would present a different kind of problem. If he looked into it and saw everything duplicated, yet not to be touched nor used, he might be filled with superstitious awe. This might be some strange object of magic. On the other hand, he might simply take it in his stride as being very like the smooth waters of a pool. Philosophers are more likely to begin wondering about the status of the objects in the mirror, and we may recall that Plato even made the status of works of art similar to the status of mirror images, that is to say, they have no status as objects in the world at all.

If we think of works of art as symbolic they have a status of their own, but it is difficult to determine the nature of this status. Some signs justify their existence solely by their reference to something else; for instance, signposts have no reason for existing apart from the giving of a direction. Now works of art, to be rightly called "symbols," must have some kind of relationship with something else, but it is not a relationship of simple direction to that other thing. They are looked at for their own sake and for the sake of their own qualities, and it is not as if the signpost, with time, had become pleasant to look at, because it would still remain true that it was not as a signpost it was pleasant to look at, but almost as a natural object. *Qua* signpost it is a pointer, and accidentally something pleasant to look at. The work of art *qua* art is both pleasant to look at *and* a pointer. It is not a pointer in the obvious sense of there being two things, one of which points to the other, but in the sense that in understanding the one thing completely, we are led to think about or dwell on a set of related images or notions. This set of images must be related in a very special sense; we must not indulge in a reverie of ideas related by the chance of our history, but rather accept the given work as guiding exactly the direction of our imagination. The nearest I can get to it is that the given object with its surface qualities is directing us to a much more complex and detailed object, which may be said to be the "meaning" of the first. This "meaning" may coincide with what the artist intended, or it may not. It is likely

that even in the case of the most articulate of artists, there is much more in what he says than even
he knew. Ambiguity, allusiveness, and, with the
most articulate, punning are the stock in trade of
the poet and prose writer, but their words may run
beyond even their awareness. However, this does
not excuse producers, such as Jonathan Miller, in
their handling of the classics—it even makes it
worse. So confident is Jonathan Miller that he has
seen something concealed from the ordinary man
that he will not let Shakespeare speak as he wishes,
with ambiguities left for his auditors to ponder, but
thrusts upon us *one* of the interpretations.

The importance of ambiguity in art may seem,
from the above description, to apply only to the
literary arts. It is, of course, to be seen most literally
in the literary arts, but even in painting one may
perceive related devices. There are paintings in
which a maiden is seen peacefully holding a sub-
dued dragon by her girdle tied around its neck,
and we do not understand it unless we know that
the artist intended a satire on the romantic story of
St. George and the Dragon. A poet may say of a
maiden, without absurdity, "Her neck was like a
swan's," but a painter could not give her a swan's
neck. He could, however, use a device such as
showing the maiden and the swan with a similar
arch, which would serve the purpose of the poet's
simile. In music, we have Wotan's presence not sus-
pected by the personages on the stage, while we,
the audience, are made aware of his presence by
the music. What I am trying to convey is the im-
mense complexity of art and the corresponding

complexity of aesthetic experience, beginning with the first impact. Here is something terrific—worth pursuing through the maze of metaphor and allusion—to a final experience, expressed in "This is the work." I say "final," but it is a relative finality. If the work were really worth pursuing, one may come back to it again and again and find more there. We may not, however, ask the artist to help us in this unraveling, or we may be met with Henry James's rejoinder to an admirer who was foolish enough to ask the Master the meaning of a certain passage in *The Wings of the Dove:* "My dear lady, if after the infinite labour I give to my literature I am unable to convey to you my meaning, how can you expect me to do so by mere word of mouth?"[8]

[8] Simon Nowell-Smith, *The Legend of the Master*, London, 1947. P. 110.

CHAPTER VI

Communication and the Artist

Our next task is to examine what artists themselves think of themselves as doing. This is a somewhat difficult notion because artists may "know" without being able to state in words what it is that they are doing. They have to suffer being told by others what they are doing. The exception, of course, is artists whose medium is words. They can retaliate, but other artists feel a dumb resentment. They either resent what is being said or feel resentment at the whole notion that what they are doing can be said in words at all. Even artists in words feel that it is unsuitable to ask them what they are doing, since what they are doing is what they have already done, as Henry James is quoted as saying so forcibly in the last chapter.

The present age has produced artists in words who not only think they know exactly what they would like to do, but expend their energies in pointing out that what they would like to do is simply impossible. They are preoccupied with what they see as the inevitable isolation of human beings from one another. They think that it is of the

utmost importance that we should not misunder-
stand one another, but with their sense of this
importance and the consequent importance of
communication go a profound and melancholy conviction that communication is never achieved.
Oddly enough, the period of doubt about the possibility of communication coincides with the period
in which the physical means of communication
have never been so efficient, so much studied, or
so well understood. The air is humming with con-
veyors of messages, radio waves, telegraph and
telephone vibrations along the wires, and our own
little contributions of sound waves as we speak and
lecture to one another. At the same time that the
physical methods of communication have reached
a pitch of perfection never approached before, we
are assailed by doubts as to whether that toward
which these methods are essentially directed ever
takes place.

Perhaps this is not so surprising as it first appears.
At first sight it would be natural to think that since
we have now mastered the technique of communication, it will go on more efficiently than ever before. On further reflection we begin to think that
what can be done so efficiently, even done by machines, is not after all what we are really concerned
with when we think of the intimate relationships
among human beings, of the exchange of confi-
dences, the sharing of experiences, and the discussion of the worth and value of human action. If a
machine teaches very efficiently, then it may be
that the time has come for human teachers to take
warning. If this is what machines do when they

teach, then perhaps some quite different service must be offered by men. Machines can give instructions, convey information, tell us when we answer questions wrongly, and set us on the right path again. What more is needed? It may seem obvious that there can be nothing in a machine comparable to the expression and evocation of emotion. Yet we hear of machines writing not only love letters, but also poetry and musical compositions, and we remember that for many people art has, as its function, to express and communicate emotion. If a poem appears to communicate emotion (I say "appears" because if *this* poem was produced by a machine, then the appearance may be illusory), then we should not feel surprised when our novelists and playwrights present human beings as simply existing side by side, soliloquizing in one another's presence rather than holding conversations with one another. The "communication" cannot be judged by appearances, for the machine-made love poem "looked like" a communication. Even here, however, our novelists and playwrights are not playing fair. If they are trying to exhibit human beings failing to communicate with one another, they should show us ordinary conversations failing to make contact instead of the very special conversations of *Waiting for Godot, The Waves,* and *The Caretaker.*

When people deny that something exists, they are not denying the facts on which belief in its existence is based, but the interpretation of those facts. People who maintain the essential separateness of human beings from one another are, after all, living

in our common world in which they, like everybody
else, buy things from shops, ask for tickets to travel
on trains and buses, and call in plumbers to mend
the pipes. So they are not denying that people can
and do give one another instructions, orders, and
information. Since the orders and information are
acted upon, or rebelled against, they have at least
been received by the other person. Such people do
not even deny that what looks like conversation between human beings takes place. What they are
denying is that by these means people are in communication with one another. What more do they
ask before they will agree that communication has
indeed taken place?

Take a case in which two people are presented
as speaking to one another. In the most extreme of
modern plays they do not all speak together, one
leaves off when the other begins and begins when
the other leaves off. At least each knows that the
other is speaking. We sometimes have cases in
which they complain that they can't "get through"
to one another. They are doing the paradoxical
thing that our novelists and playwrights are doing;
they are saying "Will you please listen to me complain that people cannot communicate with one
another."

This common metaphor is illuminating. We say
that we cannot "get through"—a complaint which
we so often have to make to the girl at the telephone exchange. The invention of the telephone
enabled us to get through to one another from far
away, where before we should have been safely
not-get-at-able, each in his own house. But it

doesn't always work. We imagine the bell pealing away in an empty house, or we have a feeling that the house is not empty, but for some reason the ringing is being ignored. For whatever reason, the physical apparatus is doing its part but we cannot "get through" to our party. This gives us the model for the modern view of human communication. I may stand before you, agitating the sound waves as I speak. They fall on your ears and set up a vibration in your brain substance, but somehow I have not gotten through. Karl Pearson used the telephone exchange metaphor to exhibit the separateness of human beings from the outside world.[1] We are each shut up in our own head, receiving messages from the outside world but never in direct contact with it. Similarly, people seem to say today that we are each shut up in our own heads, receiving only messages from our fellows, never in direct contact with them. This is, perhaps, the secret of the frightening fascination of Sidney Nolan's paintings of and the films about the legendary Australian outlaw Ned Kelly. Kelly is shown in his homemade armor, his square tin head completely blank, no holes through which messages can enter or come out. This seems to be the modern view of the true situation of men in their attempts at communication with one another.

Let us consider some cases in which communication admittedly breaks down, and then we shall be free to consider whether, these cases aside, communication has to fail even under the most favor-

---

[1] *The Grammar of Science*, London, 1937. P. 42.

able circumstances. Let us consider whether, that
is to say, there is anything at all which can count
as communication. Communication fails where two
people are speaking together, but from two very
different standpoints, social, national, or whatever.
I do not mean from two points of view represent-
ing conflicting interests; it is not communication
but agreement which fails here. I mean cases where
the hearer takes the remarks of the speaker in a
different context from that assumed by the speaker.
As frequently happens, the best examples come
from the humorists. There are P. G. Wodehouse's
two burglars who are enjoying a peaceful glass of
port after packing up the valuables in an empty
house. One of them prides himself on his knowledge of the aristocracy and their ways. Leaning
back in his chair and gazing at the light sparkling
through his glass of port he asks idly, "Who do you
think would go in to dinner first, the sister of an
earl or the daughter of a baronet?" His companion
replies from an entirely different context, "It depends who's quickest on her feet." Communication
has failed so completely here that reproaches of
commonness and ignorance from the one side
quickly lead to accusations of pretension from the
other, and their falling on one another with punches
and blows until they are collected and carted off
unconscious by the police. Except for this result,
this kind of exchange could be paralleled in many
philosophical discussions, when say, a theist is confronted by a positivist. In fact, a wary philosopher
will find out first in what context an admission will
be taken before he makes it. An exchange from the

Moral Science Club at Cambridge went as follows: A. "At least you will admit that two and two make four." B. "No I won't, not until I know what you are going to do with it."

Communication may fail where the context evoked is the same in speaker and hearer, but where the hearer lacks the experience to give content to what he hears. Unless we actually experience nostalgia we cannot understand what people are saying to us when they try to tell us about their experience when they were miles away from home. We describe to one another occasions on which we have felt homesick, but if our hearer recalls similar occasions, and reports no peculiar feeling that might be called homesickness, we cannot hope that he will understand what we are talking about. We may then resort to artists in words or sounds or colored shapes who succeed in conveying to people of normal sensibility the experience in question.

We have now reached the position that if two people wish to be sure that they are communicating with one another, they will find no real difficulty if they are giving one another pieces of information, instructions, and orders. If they wish to inform one another as to their mental state, there will be little more difficulty than if the information were about sights and sounds. If we cannot agree in the description of a certain color, we can settle the difference by bringing in a color card. A slightly more difficult case would be a dispute about the way to describe human emotions or actions. If I call *that* a case of heroism and you disagree, there is nothing comparable to the color card for us to appeal to.

Perhaps the nearest to the color card would be classical examples from history or legend, though our estimates of such cases vary with the times. Aeneas bearing his father from the burning ruins of Troy might stand as a model of filial piety, as Judas stands as the model of treachery. It is more difficult still if what we want to do is not merely to tell one another that we have had a horrifying experience, but also to convey the horror. This is where art comes in.

Let us suppose that all these difficulties have been overcome. We now feel confident that we can make one another understand that we have had certain kinds of experiences and sometimes are able to bring them to feel their peculiar emotional flavor. If all this has happened, would this be good enough? Would our modern writers accept this as successful communication? My feeling is that they would still not be satisfied, that in fact they cannot be satisfied because they are asking for a logical impossibility. For them, somebody wishing to communicate—as they would say, to be in true communication with another—is to be like Walt Disney's Harry Hare who played himself at tennis, leaping over the net so quickly that he was in time to return his own service, then back again to return his return. He wanted to be on both ends of his service and return, and in the same way our man wants to be on both ends of his messages. He knows what it feels like to send out a given message; he wants to know also what it feels like to receive it. Only so, he thinks, can two people really be in communication with one another. The only snag is that now there is no point in sending out messages. Why bother to send out messages that you yourself are to receive? Communication between persons who remain stubbornly themselves and separate is the only communication worthy of the name. What our despairing people are demanding as perfect communication is the destruction of its essential condition.

At this point we may notice that our requirements make communication a work of art as well as making a work of art a communication; and if art is thought of as self-expression, then self-expression necessarily goes along with communication. It is usually assumed that each man is acquainted at least with himself, but it seems to me that the process of becoming acquainted with oneself necessarily goes along with the process of becoming acquainted with another person. If I never exchange remarks with anybody else, never have any dealings with or evoke a response from him, I do not really know what my emotions are. We say of someone who utters a spiteful remark, "He must be jealous." Equally and with the same shock of surprise we feel a pang when we hear of a friend's success and say, "I must be jealous." The difference between the two cases is that in the first we heard the spiteful remark while the friend had the pang; in the second case, we had the pang but this led us to say, just as hearing the remark led us to say of our friend, "I, the person who had the pang, must be jealous," not "am jealous" but "must be." It is an inference in both cases. It seems to be assumed that the self that remains stubbornly mine, and

from which others are inescapably cut off, is a con-
geries of such pangs, flashes of hopefulness, feelings
of nostalgia. Certainly our growing knowledge of
and acquaintance with our companions and the
world has a running accompaniment to such feelings; but what makes us separate from yet interested in one another is not that running accompaniment but that which is accompanied. It is our
growing knowledge of the world, each from his
own point of view, our changing and developing
attitudes toward it, and our own peculiar methods
of dealing with it. It is this that makes communication necessary, possible, and worthwhile.

A further paradox arises from our demand to be
in direct and complete communication with one
another, to feel one another's feelings and think
one another's thoughts. Let us take an example first
of an attempt to enter completely into the concerns
of another person in which it is easier to exhibit
the paradox, and then go on to the attempt to take
up one another's thoughts, feelings, and attitudes
toward the external world.

A and B each wishes to demonstrate his tender
concern for the other. A says, "I worry only about
your worries, B." B says, "I worry only about your
worries, A." In that case, neither has any worries,
although A has headaches and an overdraft at the
bank, and B has a weak chest and chilblains. They
see this to be absurd, and each amends his position. A says, "I worry about all our worries, both
yours and mine." B says the same, but now they
have too many worries. A worries not only about
B's weak chest, but about B's worry about his weak

chest, and this constitutes a new worry for A and consequently a new worry for B, and so on indefinitely. They see this to be as absurd as the first state and agree on the following amendment. The tender concern of each for the other is to be shown reasonably by concern for all the ills of both, that is to say, each will feel his own first-order worry. The second-order worry for the feelings of worry of the other will be a matter of concern only if it constitutes a first-order worry, i.e., A might be worried about B's tendency to worry about his chilblains as a sign of bad circulation and so of a weak heart.

Let us now draw a parallel to this case, in the mutual desire of A and B each to feel what the other feels toward their common world. They stand in A's garden, which is bedded out with scarlet geraniums, blue lobelias, and white marguerites. B hates it, and thinks his own arrangement of delphiniums, heliotrope, and pink rambler roses is much to be preferred. He stands and looks at A's red, white, and blue, trying to feel A's delight in it, but A is trying to feel B's dislike of it. It is a hopeless case since neither is feeling his usual feeling for what he sees, and so neither has anything to communicate to the other. Their first amendment leads them to admit first-order feelings. Each must hang on to his primary feeling, A of delight in his flower arrangement and his deprecation of B's dislike of it, but he has now presented a new feeling to B, namely his deprecation of B's feeling, and B will now have a new feeling about his feeling, and so on. They now reach the third and reasonable position. Each must be allowed to feel his own pri-

vate feeling toward his own things; each can tell
the other *that* they feel in a certain way toward
those things. A can understand that his feeling for
his red, white, and blue resembles B's feeling for
his pink, blue, and mauve, but if each feels the
other's feeling for these diverse objects there is no
longer an A-ish state for B to become aware of, or
a B-ish state for A to become aware of. Plotinus
said that if individual souls were not separate and
distinct we should all experience one another's sensations, desires, and thoughts, even everything that
occurred in the universe.[2] (This of course assumes
that there are no unoccupied points of view, which
may be allowed to pass if we include the omni-
presence of God.) In either event it would mean in
effect that there were no points of view, since whatever was experienced from any point of view
would be experienced from every point of view.

Having established, I hope, that communication
does as a matter of fact take place, it remains to
show in what particular way art performs this function. There are several related notions—art as expression, as symbolic, as communication, and as
language. They are not identical notions; we could
express ourselves without our meaning being com-
prehended by our hearer, art could be symbolic
without succeeding in being understood, we could
do our half of communication and not be received,
but if we speak of art as language then quite definitely it could not be language unless we shared it
with others and unless it were hypothetically un-

[2] *Ennead IV*, trans. Stephen MacKenna and B. S. Page,
London, 1927-30. Section 3.

derstandable even if not understood by them. What is common to these notions is that all of them are human activities, making use of the means common to us all as human beings. If we express ourselves or make use of symbols, it is in the terms that other people, at least those in our community, will also use. If we express ourselves and look at the result, if we were to try to perfect what we had said, our corrections would be to make the result clearer, more lucid, i.e., to show it more clearly to our companions. The difference between speaking of art as "expression" and of art as "language" lies in the attention we are giving to our audience. It may be that an artist is chiefly concerned to make his own incoherent and chaotic state clear to himself, but in the very act of making it clear to himself by the means that he shares in common with his fellows, he is also making it clear to them.

The most important difference between the aestheticians who think of art as expression and those who prefer the metaphor of language lies in what would constitute the excellence of art in the two cases. Aestheticians tend to assume that success in the aim of art necessarily brings about beauty. For instance, Croce and his followers, the most notable of whom in England is R. G. Collingwood,[3] assume that if an artist succeeds in making absolutely and utterly and minutely clear what he is experiencing, he has necessarily produced a valuable object. Somebody who thinks of art as language will think that the artist has succeeded only if he has man-

[3] *Principles of Art,* Oxford, 1947. P. 287.

aged to convey to another person what he has thought and felt. It is true that if the expression has been completely successful, then another person would be able to "get it," but that is not essential. It is no accident that for Croce and Collingwood it is not even a necessity for the artist to produce a physical object. What is of value in the making of art is the process of articulation itself. The making of an object, such as a picture, a statue, a poem, or a play, is an extra-artistic activity willed by the artist in order to remind himself of and enable him to re-create his experience. If he is a kindly man, it is also in order to enable his less gifted fellows to create an experience similar to his own.

It is interesting to notice that the very people who do the work with their hands and might be thought of as likely to repudiate the notion that the making of the work of art is in the imagination are anxious to emphasize that the experience of appreciation is of the same kind as the experience of making. They insist that the spectator constructs the work in the important sense, just as the maker constructed the work. The work done with the hands is the non-essential, what is done in the imagination is what really matters. Artists seem to agree among themselves that the difference between them and non-artists is not that they can make while others cannot, but that they can see and others do not.

There is an odd corollary to this position. Since the valuable activity takes place in the mind, there are no important distinctions to be made between kinds of art. To express oneself by means of pigments, or perhaps I should say by colored shapes, rather than by sounds is not to make an important distinction. To stress this distinction is just as silly as if one were to say "Did he express his kindly feeling by cups of tea or whisky and soda?"

There is some support for this view when one remembers that unworldly artists need no more of their writings or paintings than the making of them. We hear of canvases being salvaged from the roofs of chicken runs and practical friends collecting sheets of manuscript from the floor where they have been thrown down as being of no further value. It is quite clear on the one hand that the artist has had all he wants of them when he has made them. It is also clear that very many artists are good businessmen and know very well what to do with their work from a practical point of view. This is, however, quite a different matter. As Plato pointed out many hundreds of years ago,[4] a good shepherd studies how to care for sheep and not how to sell the wool in the best market. He is a shepherd when he cares for the sheep, and a man of business when he sells the wool. Similarly, the artist is an artist—here I was about to fall into my own trap, I was about to say he is an artist when he paints a picture, but this will not do. He is an artist when the picture is complete and finished in every detail in his imagination. He is a kindly man when he puts it on canvas and a man of business when he sells it.

There is a more difficult kind of objection than

[4] *Republic,* trans. J. L. Davies and D. J. Vaughan, Cambridge, 1886. Bk. 1, pp. 25 ff.

the difficulty of placing the value of a work of art. It lies in the relation of what we may call the "medium" to the act of creation. May we speak of the "medium" of a work that is to be completed entirely in the imagination? Croce thinks that we can —in fact he thinks that he can give a better account of the relation of the medium to the work than someone who insists on the physical making of a physical object. For him it is not a question of designing an urn and thinking, "Shall I make it in bronze or marble?" but in the very thinking, the urn is imagined as in bronze and suitably in bronze rather than in marble. He thinks that in this way every element of the finished article is suited to every other. As in so many other aesthetic theories, there is one interpretation springing immediately to the mind that runs absolutely counter to another. At first it seems as though a non-artist might say, "If it is imagining, anybody can do it. I can imagine paintings, vases, plays, and musical compositions. The difficulty is in making the thing." This is not so at all. We only think we have imagined these things, because we do not understand that imagining must be complete in every detail—in fact, to imagine it is to complete it. The counterinterpretation, far from allowing the ordinary man to think that if only he had the manual skill he could make all these beautiful objects, is harder on the ordinary man. If he has not been able to make, then he hasn't had the imagining. It is not the case that if only he had a little more skill he could have done this, that, and the other, but if he could do all these things he would have had the skill. There are no "mute inglorious Miltons"; if they are mute, they are not Miltons.

For expression theory, the only artistic virtue is sincerity and the only vice, the lie in the soul. One may choose to falsify in the actual writing down or painting, but to refuse to accept and make clear what is found in oneself is to produce non-art. This insincerity is detected as a defect in the work or as ruling out the work as art altogether.

The contrast between art as expression and as communication lies in a different context, in the estimation of the success of the work. Unless we insist that communication has taken place only if the artist has completely and honestly laid bare his inner state, the artist can communicate anything he chooses. The success lies in the extent to which he has conveyed to the hearer (in the case of verbal communication) what he intended him to understand. There would be no particular reason why he should not wish to communicate his own disguised state to his hearer. There is no demand on the artist to lay bare his innermost thoughts if we are simply thinking of art as communication. However, it might be argued that to communicate falsely is not to communicate. If I always speak falsely, then the very purpose of speaking is lost. To speak is only to make noises, if it is not usually done in order to convey facts or to express emotion. Art, however, is in a different category. I do not think anybody would wish to say that if an artist did not speak truly he was frustrating his own efforts. If I am in simple communication with my fellows, then I am expected to tell the truth, but if I am making an object with artifice then I may have quite a different purpose from that of speaking the simple truth. The same applies to the making of works of art as symbols. To make a symbol is to choose an object that will present to another person what I had in mind to show him when I made it. This is not necessarily my own state. The important difference between thinking of art as expression and thinking of art as the making of an object that will serve to communicate or to act as a symbol is that expression is not expression unless it is of what truly is.

Having established, to my own satisfaction at least, that it is a logical absurdity to deny that the conditions for communication exist—after all, how can we deplore non-communication if according to our own account the conditions for communication never occur—we may now go on to examine the most obvious kind of communication. There is no doubt that if communication between human beings takes place, it is most likely to be by means of language, and there is a traditional aesthetic theory according to which *art* is language. It is rarely left at the unconditional statement that art is language, but that art is the language of the emotions. Professor E. H. Gombrich examines this notion very carefully in a paper delivered to a meeting of the Aristotelian Society, but it is my contention that his analysis fits art considered as language *about* emotion, not art as the language *of* the emotions. His examples are all of communication of the *fact* of emotion, but I hope to show in the succeeding pages that to communicate the fact of emotion is not to communicate emotion.

Before coming to an examination of Professor Gombrich's position, it is essential to say something of the theory of art as the language of the emotions in relation to the literary arts. The difficulty here is that we have a double-order of language. There is no doubt that poets, playwrights, and novelists use words and the words they use are the words that we non-artists use in our everyday conversations and communications with our fellows. (This is not to say however, that "le bourgeois gentilhomme" was right when he thought he had discovered that he had been talking prose all his life!) What then can be meant by speaking of the literary arts as presenting works that use "the language of the emotions"? Professor William Empson devotes several pages to an analysis of the line: "Bare ruined choirs where late the sweet birds sang."[5] I do not propose to enter into the question of the arrogance of supposing that I or any other ordinary person could present a paraphrase of this evocative and allusive line. I simply say that looking at a row of elm trees with abandoned nests, I might say, "In the spring we used to hear the birds singing in chorus from those trees." Now I have made a plain statement of fact. This plain statement might evoke an emotional response in you, but this response will arise not from my choice of words but from the state of affairs to which I am directing your attention. Art— here, poetry—is the language of the emotions in the sense that it is evoking in you not the simple response to the state of affairs described, but the re-

[5] *Seven Types of Ambiguity*, London, 1953. P. 2.

sponse to the state of affairs as related to many
other similar situations, sets of words, and joys,
which if evoked by my simple words would have
been your own imaginative construction. What
Shakespeare has given us is a controlled system of
images leading to a unified and harmonious whole.
We read Shakespeare's line as though it were twice
removed from reality—mine as once removed. My
line referred directly to the facts—Shakespeare's, to
a reaction to the facts. In the same sense, we "read"
a painting, i.e., what we see is to be interpreted,
and we read a poem, i.e., what we hear is also to be
interpreted.

We may now return to Professor Gombrich.
What we are given in his paper "Art and the Language of the Emotions" is an ingenious account of
parallel scales with variations on each combining
with variations on another, to make clear a dominant emotion modified in various ways. In his *Art
and Illusion* we are shown how pictures should
be read from clues yielded by our knowledge of
the traditional conventions—for example,
means a castle. There is a fundamental defect in
Professor Gombrich's account of the "reading" of
pictures, when one remembers that his account of
perception of the natural world parallels his account of the perception of pictures. We read our
firsthand experience as we read art. Professor Gombrich used the following illustration: Given
the clue, this is easily seen as a giraffe passing a
window, otherwise, it might be seen as footprints

on a path in the snow. The defect is that if everything is seen as a sign of something else—for example, if is seen as a castle at a distance in the natural landscape and as a picture of a castle at a certain time in art history, then when is ever seen just as itself? It would seem to follow that nothing is ever simply seen, but always *seen as*. It is hard then to understand how we arrive at the notion of simply seeing when all we have ever experienced is "seeing as."

What is more to our point, however, is Professor Gombrich's excellent account in his paper in the *Proceedings of the Aristotelian Society*, Supplementary Volume, 1962, of the system of associated scales of color, shape, texture, sound, etc., that may give rise to the most complicated patterns of heaviness in color with lightness of texture, lightness of touch with depth of sound, yielding delight in the allusive and punning works of art and giving rise to delicately adjusted systems of emotion. However this is not, from my point of view, to establish art as specifically the language of the emotions. I quote in full Professor Gombrich's final example because for me it brings out its fatal defect. I must first, however, emphasize that Professor Gombrich is not committing himself here or elsewhere to the theory that art is the language of the emotions, but setting out how art would work if it *were* the language of the emotions. Here is his example:

. . . Let us think of a correspondent who regularly writes letters overseas at the present postage rate of sixpence. One day, in a receptive state of mind, he is struck by the prosy purple colour of the sixpenny stamp and, being in a playful mood, he casts around for other combinations that would express his feelings more adequately. Needless to say, the recipient might never notice this deviation from the norm if he were not told of the birth of a new art form. But once the stage is set, our players could start the game. Their medium consists of ten denominations of stamps—½d., orange; 1d., blue; 1½d., green; 2d., brown; 2½d., red; 3d., purple; 4d., light blue; 4½d., light red; 5d., light brown; 6d., light purple. Both financial prudence and a sense of form impose the rule of affixing the right amount. Even within this limiting rule, however, there are no less than six choices of uniform colours (12 orange, 6 blue, 4 green, 3 brown, 2 purple, 1 light purple) which may reflect quite a variety of moods—"reflect," that is, for the partner who would appreciate the message of three brown stamps as about the drabbest that could be selected. Given such a partner, he would surely and rightly expect a splendid piece of news when he saw the envelope decorated with the maximum of variety, one orange, say, one blue, one red, one green, then another orange, keeping the contrasts throughout at the widest. Combine the two oranges and go thence to red and then from blue to green, and the tension has subsided although the mood is still very bright.

Of course, the two can also agree on the direction of reading, making the left-hand stamp the "classifier" that stands for the dominant mood, while the others articulate it in succession. Perhaps great anger and some sadness would lead to two red, and one blue stamp. Only a fit of reckless fury, however, would break through the rules altogether and affix three red stamps to the gratuitous expense of 1½d. But in such a fit of extreme expressionist abandon, our correspondent would be in danger of spoiling his medium for good. Once the rule is broken, there is no valid reason why he should not plaster the whole envelope with colours. Moreover, going back to the rules will be increasingly difficult, for it would not imply that his emotions have cooled more than he would like to indicate. As a true artist, therefore, our correspondent will not yield to this temptation of "breaking the form," at least till he has exhausted all its possibilities. What challenges his imagination is rather the game itself, the wealth of combinations adding up to sixpence which the reader is invited to explore. Perhaps those who get really absorbed in the game will try to fit their moods in interesting combinations rather than make the message fit the mood. Only those who do, I believe, may have the true artistic temperament—but that is a different story.[6]

Professor Gombrich's discussion is a welcome attempt to take the description of art as the language

[6] "Art and the Language of the Emotions," *Proceedings of the Aristotelian Society*, Supplementary Volume, 1962.

of the emotions seriously and to work out a scheme for implementing it.[7] Nevertheless, the description seems to me to remain a metaphor, and even, perhaps, not the most satisfactory of metaphors. It is very attractive, and its attraction seems to lie in its ability to explain a puzzling and undeniable feature of art and its appreciation. There is no doubt that a work of art presents itself as containing, in some sense of the word, much more than appears on the surface. At first sight, this is a ridiculous thing to say; if there is one thing that is sure about art, it is that it is for sensuous apprehension and appreciation. It is sensible to say "They preferred to be good rather than to seem good," nonsensical to say "They preferred to be rather than to seem beautiful." Being and seeming beautiful can be distinguished only at a sophisticated level. Similarly, on the side of appreciation, it seems as though it ought to be a simple matter of looking or listening, but what we find in fact is that a work of art sets going in us a complicated system of thinking. Sherlock Holmes amazed his friend Dr. Watson by breaking in on his reverie with, "Yes, Watson, I agree—it is a preposterous way of settling disputes." He had followed Watson's reverie, from his reading of a newspaper paragraph, to a glance at a portrait of General Gordon, a hint of being troubled by an old

[7] The remainder of this chapter is my considered response to Professor Gombrich's paper, which appeared with his in the *Proceedings of the Aristotelian Society*, Supplementary Volume, 1962. There will be some repetition of points already made, but I have chosen to include my entire paper since it constitutes my view of what art must do to be rightly considered as a language of the emotions.

wound, to the recognition of the futility of war. Holmes read his friend, as we say, "like a book." In *Art and Illusion,* Professor Gombrich invited us to read pictures like a book, and I do not mind committing myself to the paradoxical assertion that Professor Empson reads poetry "like a book."

This account of art and its appreciation suffers from the defect that if we are to "read the signs," what is there is there not for its own sake and for the sake of its sensible properties, but for its meaning. In his paper Professor Gombrich seems to me to have become aware of this defect and to be supplementing his former account with a description which takes notice of the directly evocative power of the actual colors and shapes in paintings. How far he succeeds in avoiding the central difficulty of the metaphor of art as language remains to be considered, but if he has done nothing else, he has given a satisfactory account of the activity aroused in spectators when confronted with a work of art and of the correlation between the elements of the experience and the elements of the work. With this introduction, I take up my task by examining what must be said about a "language of the emotions" and how it is to be applied in our description of art. I shall then return to what I take to be the true nature of Professor Gombrich's achievement.

To communicate information about things is straightforward, since we are referring one another to common objects that we can examine together. To communicate information about our sensible experiences is less satisfactory, since once again we have to refer one another to common objects and rely on the similarity of our sense organs to ensure that communication has been achieved. To communicate information about our emotional experiences is one stage further removed from straightforward talk about objects, since differences in temperament, history, mood, etc. prevent us from assuming a degree of similarity of emotional response comparable to the similarity of our sensible responses. The two latter cases are complicated if we refer one another to objects as possessing the sensible or emotion-arousing properties. People stubbornly maintain that the rain-water butt is green though it has long faded to a mossy gray, and I shall not even attempt an illustration of difference in emotional response to the same object, so varied are human beings in this respect. The color card and scales of various kinds are devices for stabilizing reports of sensible experience, and Professor Gombrich's suggestions might be followed up to give us a device for stabilizing reports of emotional response. We could have an emotion card, bearing a set of colored shapes ringing the changes on combinations of colors, shapes, and intensities, correlated with blends and intensities of emotions. Since size would also matter—we could not have a tiny rage—we could not manage a uniform set of emotion cards, but we could have a gallery, each emotion in its proper size. But this would only be to give content to our emotion words so that we could make statements conveying information about emotion, just as the color card gives content to our statements about color experiences. *This* is what I mean by crimson—*this* is what I mean by melancholy. What we have provided is a referent for "melancholy," i.e., the emotion experienced by normal people on looking at this combination of colored shapes. With Professor Gombrich's proviso in mind, that the specific device used must be taken in relation to the range of devices available to its user, we should have to have a gallery of emotions for each century. This is eighteenth-century melancholy; this is nineteenth-century elation.

Our situation is now this. Just as we sample a new dish, allowing a portion to remain on our tongues while we savor it, tracking down each separate flavor, so, when we wish to communicate information about our emotional state, we savor it, tracking down here a general resentment, there a flickering generosity. Then we are in a position to make a report. The trouble here is that there seems to be no special difficulty. We do not need a special language of the emotions; our ordinary language does well enough, with some device for giving content to our emotion words. But people obviously feel some special difficulty about communicating emotion or they would not say that this is the peculiar function of art. The difficulty comes at us from two sides. On the one hand, people feel that communicating information *about* emotion is not good enough. If I have had a terrible nightmare, it is not enough that I should make you believe that it was horrible, I want you to feel its horror. When the White King says, "The horror of that moment I shall never forget," and the White Queen replies, "You will, unless you make a memorandum of it," we take this for a joke, because we know that a memorandum, "had a horrible experience," would never be enough to recall what we wish to recall—the horror and not merely the fact that it was horrible.

A language of the emotions, then, is not a language devised to convey information about emotions and here Professor Gombrich's examples do him less than justice. Theseus' black sail conveyed the false information that the expedition had failed. It happened that the way chosen to convey this piece of information was specially suitable in view of the way the king expected to feel toward it. Here our difficulty comes at us from the other side. Just as we felt that communicating information about emotion was not good enough, so we feel that there is a mode of experience which, to put it mildly, *is* good enough to communicate emotion. (Here we must be careful. Hamlet feels himself obliged to say: " 'Tis not alone my inky cloak, good mother,/ Nor customary suits of solemn black . . ./That can denote me truly: these indeed seem,/For they are actions that a man might play:/But I have that within which passeth show;/These but the trappings and the suits of woe." Hamlet wishes to do two things—to express his grief and respect for his father, though he has no hope of communicating it, and to communicate the fact, as a reproach to his mother, that here is true mourning for the late king.) What is decidedly and undoubtedly "good enough" in the attempts of human beings to communicate their emotional states to one another is the whole world of poetry, plays, music, painting, dancing, and sculpture.

Is, then, to communicate emotion simply to communicate information about emotion in a specially suitable manner? For example, A tells B that he is unhappy in such words that B feels unhappy. I must not say that B feels unhappy *too*, for A might be such a master of language that he makes B unhappy while he himself has felt little or nothing. He would, then, not have *communicated* emotion but aroused it. Similarly, if A is angry and his expression of rage frightens B, then again he has not communicated but aroused emotion. If A is mourning his lost love and so comports himself that B becomes melancholy too and begins to mourn his wasted youth, then A has infected B with melancholy, but he has not communicated it to him. If A composes and plays a nostalgic tune while thinking of his childhood in the Alps and B, listening, engages in reverie about his home on the prairies, then the emotions are similar, but each is so tied up with its object that no communication of emotion can be said to have taken place. A communicates emotion to B in these circumstances: A makes an object, visible or audible, that seems to him an appropriate expression of his emotional state, presents it to B who takes it as the appropriate correlate of the emotional state into which it causes him to pass. A and B each assumes that he is experiencing an emotion similar to the other's. If it were possible to pluck an emotion from my heart and plant it in yours, this would be the complete and unambiguous communication of emotion, and the above is the nearest we can come to it. It may of course never happen, and it could not be known for sure whether it had happened or not, but that it does happen is the presupposition of calling art the "language of the emotions."

But is "language" the suitable word to use in describing what happens? If I use language, i.e., marks or sounds with meaning, I am presenting the marks or sounds not for you to look at or listen to but to "look through" at the meaning. If I upbraid you, I shall have failed in my use of language if you listen to the flow of words admiringly and say, "What a command of invective!" or "How the rising and falling cadences match the anger and regret!" Roger Fry remarked that, biologically speaking, art is a blasphemy.[8] Perception and emotion are for the sake of action, not contemplation. We might add that, described as language, art is a semantic blasphemy. Signs are for directing our attention to something else, not to their own sensible properties.

Reynolds makes us aware of this problem. He too used the metaphor of language, but, speaking of the ornamental style of the Venetian School, he grants them a mastery of the language of painting but goes on to say, "It is but poor eloquence which only shows that the orator can talk. Words should be employed as the means, not as the end."[9] The language of painting is "the power of drawing, modelling, and using colours," and this power may be acquired by the practice of copying faithfully any object placed before one. There are, then, no

[8] *Vision and Design*, London, 1920. P. 47.
[9] *Discourses*, "The Fourth Discourse," ed. Roger Fry, London, 1905. P. 87.

visible marks that function both as literal parts of
the painting and as signs of something beyond
themselves, that is to say, there is no vocabulary.
What Reynolds is describing as "language" is more
properly grammar, i.e., a system of principles guiding the putting together of parts that are not to be
looked on as signs but as there for their own sake.

Fry points out the inconsistency of this account
of language with Reynolds' recommendation to
young painters to form a close acquaintance with
the works of the masters. He says: "The artist of
the Renaissance never learned the grammar that
Reynolds presupposes. For by this correct drawing
of any object is meant an indifferent exactitude, a
passionless and disinterested précis of facts—in
short, an unartistic drawing. Now, the artist of the
Renaissance learned first an artistic formula, the
formula of his time as understood by his master,
and this became so much of a second nature to
him that when he looked at Nature he saw it in
terms of his formula."[10]

Fry's use of "language" here is that of Professor
Gombrich's *Art and Illusion* but not of his paper,
for as we noticed before Professor Gombrich also
has a double account of art as language in order to
avoid our dilemma. In *Art and Illusion* the account
demands conventional signs, i.e., literal marks that
are to be read or taken as clues; but in his paper the
marks are "natural signs," i.e., to be taken, not read.
This dilemma comes out clearly in Professor Gombrich's postage stamp illustration taken in conjunc-

[10] *Ibid.*, "Introduction to the Twelfth Discourse," p. 319.

tion with his own illuminating comment on it in his final sentence. The illustration fails to describe art, since the blaze of color on the envelope refers us to and stands or falls by its appropriateness to the contents of the envelope. In the illustration, the pattern of colored stamps was a sign of good news inside. The recipient would have had a grievance if the news inside had been of things going on in the same way. But he might be so delighted with the blaze of color that he simply looks and enjoys, just as in the last sentence the maker of the pattern became so intrigued that he did not bother with the news it had to signal. It has now become art, but has ceased to mean. Professor Gombrich cannot have it both ways: either the blaze of color is not a signal of good news or it is not art. However, this is only an illustration, and we will now look at the theory anew in the light of our account of what it means to communicate emotion.

To repeat: A communicates emotion to B when A produces an audible or visible object, using "object" very widely to cover a pattern of sounds as in the reading of a poem or the playing of a piece of music, which A offers as an appropriate expression of his emotion and which B takes in the same way, i.e., B feels a similar emotion to that of A in respect of the same object and sees the emotion as appropriate. Now we have to answer two questions— first, as to the kind of emotion in general that could be so communicated, and second, as to the place in A's history that the specific emotion or set of emotions holds. The two answers have bearing on one another, because the answer to the first question is that, without reference to a common object, the only emotion that could be aroused would be one belonging to a general state, such as melancholy, elation, or bitterness, and not love, hatred, or jealousy. If the latter kind of emotion is to be communicated, then it must be emotion directed toward everyday objects or events, the perception of which so excited the artist that he set to work on, possibly, their representation or on some object related to them in some other way.

The romantic notion of art as communicating emotion is that the artist embodies the emotions aroused in him by the stimulating or originating experience in an object that directly arouses similar emotions in his spectator-audience and toward "his" objects. It is said that everyone has it in him to write one novel. This dictum expresses this romantic notion. It is based on the common feeling of nostalgia toward one's childhood environment and experience. Everyone, it is thought, has enough and powerful enough remembered emotion to render these experiences in a form so suited to them that the resulting work must convey just these emotionally colored experiences to the reader. This may be so. It may be that anyone who can write at all, if called on to write the story of his childhood, would be so stimulated that the book would be evocative to any reader. Lyrical poetry seems to have this evocative power, but it cannot be said of every form of art, and not of all lyrical poetry. It is much more valid to say that an artist in words is someone who could not fail to write a novel about his childhood experiences.

As soon as we make this modification, the situation is radically altered. It is no longer the emotionally colored originating experience that has to be conveyed, but the experience as seen by an artist. Richard Wagner expresses the situation exactly in *A Happy Evening*. He writes: "When a musician feels prompted to sketch the smallest composition, he owes it simply to the stimulus of a feeling that usurps his whole being at the hour of conception. This mood may be brought about by an outward experience or have arisen from a secret inner spring; whether it shows itself as melancholy, joy, desire, contentment, love, or hatred, in the musician it will always take a musical shape, and voice itself in tones or ever it is cast in notes. . . . These greater moods, as deep suffering of soul or potent exaltation, may date from outer causes, for we are all men . . . ; but *when* they force the musician to production, these greater moods have already turned to music in him."[11] Such an account meets the common but shallow objection that if art is the language of the emotions, an artist cannot communicate melancholy unless he is himself melancholy all the time he is at work. What the *artist* communicates is not the melancholy of the originating ex-

---

[11] *A Happy Evening*, Paris, 1841. *A Happy Evening in Paris* originally appeared in two parts in the *Gazette Musicale* in Paris in October and November 1841. The copies in the British Museum Reading Room were destroyed in the blitz. Ernest Newman in his *Life of Richard Wagner* (Vol. 1, page 276) says that *A Happy Evening in Paris* was included by Wagner in the collected edition of his literary works published in the 1870s. I have not been able to see this collection.

perience, but the excitement of matching melancholy with sound, words, or colors. If it be objected that it must then have ceased to be melancholy, the answer is that melancholy must remain as an element, or the process described by Wagner could not go on. It must remain, too, as an element in the process of correcting that goes on in the course of the work. In the light of what does the artist change a word, remove a line, tone down a color? Some people describe this process in terms of an imagined whole that the artist has before his mind's eye or ear. Some describe it in terms of a desired unity in the work as it shapes itself under his eye. But why does he desire such unity, or why, sometimes, does he desire to introduce a discordant note? The answer, in terms of our theory of communication, is that alteration is in the interest of adequacy. Is *this* good enough for the original exciting experience as it presented itself to the artist's perceiving eye? Our theory also provides an answer to the question of how it is possible to enjoy sad and even repulsive themes. What we are enjoying is the artist's delight in his power to match these themes. The emotion communicated is not merely Constable's love for the wide skies and flat fields of Suffolk, but his joy in seeing these loved scenes in terms of painterly composition, his feeling for what he can do with all the traditional and conventional means at his command.

One kind of emotion that an artist may feel toward his object presents us with a problem. Suppose that the originating experience were such as moved Picasso when he painted "Guernica." If our theory holds, passionate indignation must arise in the spectator or delight in the powerful delineation of a passionately hated object. Somehow, the latter description does not seem so satisfactory in this case. Some people meet the problem by noting that time must pass before such works can be viewed aesthetically, but to others this would imply that the meaning of the work had been lost. We may usefully compare "Guernica" with Breughel's "Massacre of the Innocents," in which the painter expressed his horror and indignation against the massacre of the people of the Netherlands by the Duke of Alva. This now belongs to the past, and we may ask ourselves whether we have lost or gained in our appreciation of the work. Is our reaction to "Guernica" in the white heat of the moment the model or is it the calmer enjoyment of a later time? Van Gogh once said that there were canvases that would retain their calm even in an earthquake. If we accept this as an expression of high approval, then great works either do not communicate emotion or communicate only the calm emotions, and in either case, a simple theory of art as the language of the emotions will not do.

We must now see how a theory of colored shapes, ringing the changes on combinations of shade, intensity, and shape and acting as signs of emotion, will work. There are four possibilities: (a) The painter's brush moves freely and spontaneously in the right kind of brushwork and color when he is moved and the spectator naturally responds with a similar emotion to the resulting composition. It would be difficult to describe this process for the

art of language. The relations throughout are simply causal. (b) The painter deliberately matches
his emotionally colored perception with the right
strokes and colors and the spectator responds naturally. Here, the painter is deliberately aiming at
bringing about an effect, but not at being "understood." (c) The painter naturally makes the right
strokes in the right colors and the spectator deliberately takes them as signs and reads them. This is
one-sided again, and will not do for verbal communication. (d) Both painter and spectator act deliberately—the one to communicate and the other
to accept and interpret the signs. This seems to be
the only case comparable to using language. The
connection between the experiences of artist and
spectator, the likelihood that they will resemble one
another, lies not only in the common object, but
also in the common inheritance of the tradition of
painting and of looking both at paintings and at
natural objects.

There are two objections to this account that
arise in our generation, but that would not have
troubled the people of an earlier period. The first
is that we have now been made free of the art of
people whose traditions and manner of life are unknown to us, because it is unlikely that the emotions they felt would be similar to those with which
we experience their work. Here we can only fall
back on the notion of the artist as a construction out
of his work. Even when we know quite a lot about
the life of an artist, the entity we construct out of
his work is not likely to be psychologically correct,
and it matters little that it is not.

The second objection is that in much modern work there is nothing that could be described as the "originating experience." Our only common object is the painting itself, and if emotion is to be communicated, it can be nothing but the emotion generated in the course of making this object. However, this might well be thought to be enough to fit the theory.

All that I have attempted so far is to show that it is not impossible to give a description of art as communicating emotion. This is not the only function of art and even when it happens, it does not follow that art is language. Certainly, it seems that a system of natural signs will not serve as language. "Natural" is opposed to "conventional," so that to shout "Fire!" is to use language, but to puff smoke out is to give a natural sign of fire. Smoke is a natural sign of fire in that when we see it, we may infer the presence of fire. We can hardly apply this to color, that is to say, we cannot say it is a natural sign of emotion. Suppose we say that color C, with all the modifications of shape and intensity d, e, f, and our knowledge of the resources open to the artist, is a sign of emotion E with modifications p, q, r arising from d, e, f. Does it mean that if we see C (d, e, f) we may infer E (p, q, r)? We do not need to infer it in ourselves for it will be open to inspection, but that the emotion is seen to be the *effect* of C does not allow us to infer that E will also be its cause.

What Professor Gombrich has achieved is not an analysis and implementation of art as language of the emotions; rather he has provided an apparatus and a method, if supplemented by his work in *Art and Illusion,* comparable to that of Professor Empson in his critical analysis of poetry. People like to speculate about what would surprise a Martian coming to earth with no knowledge of our life and culture. One of the things that might surprise him would be our habit of looking fixedly for a long time at a thing hanging on a wall or a small collection of folded paper. At first sight there is a disproportion between cause and effect when we look at pictures or read poetry; the mere looking leads to our being moved to emotionally colored intellectual activity. In his paper Professor Gombrich explains this apparent disproportion by analyzing the visible object and by correlating the elements with aspects of the viewer's experience. This is not to show that art is a language of any kind. What makes us think of it as language is that the critical work reveals the object as much more complex, allusive, and evocative of feeling than it at first appeared. The word which immediately springs to mind is "significant," but like most of the words we use to describe art, it is paradoxical; significant, but of nothing, unless the object on first sight is taken to be significant of the object as it presents itself after critical analysis. When Professor Empson takes several pages to set out what he gets from the line "Bare ruined choirs where late the sweet birds sang," it might be said that he was setting out its meaning, but he has wasted his time if the meaning is a set of ideas, events, or objects *outside* the line to which we are being referred. A critic's work must continually be tested by our coming back from him

to the painting or poem. If we continually apprehend the work more completely as a complex individual, then he has done his work well. In his paper and in *Art and Illusion*, Professor Gombrich
has given us the apparatus for such critical work,
but not an analysis of art as language.

Criticism such as Empson's works on two levels,
and here Gombrich's analysis is very illuminating.
A film producer, speaking of the film *Last Year in
Marienbad*, compared films to music in that "both
affect our emotions directly, not *via* the intellect."
The immediate impact of a painting may well be
of this direct kind, together with an awareness of
much to be discovered in later viewings. The language metaphor is more fittingly used in these later
explorations, since we ourselves are then reading
the signs. A critic observing our looking at paintings might also use our reactions for himself in his
account of what the painting effected in us directly.
It would be exciting to discover that for Professor
Gombrich painting too "aspires to the condition of
music"!

CHAPTER VII

The Judgment of Taste

We now come to what is usually called the judgment of taste—that is, the judgment passed upon a certain object that it is or is not beautiful. It seems desirable at this point to say something about the question whether or not this is a useful topic for aesthetic consideration and whether it is a judgment that is ever made, as a matter of fact, in its simple form. I agree at once with my inevitable critics that such an expression is hardly ever used. (As we noticed before, the late Professor J. L. Austin wished that aestheticians would concern themselves with the dainty and the dumpy rather than with the beautiful and the ugly.) However, the actual form of words used seems to me to be irrelevant. It might be "This is it," "This is the real thing," or whatever happens to be the current expression of approval. Just so long as that which all these expressions are being used for is to attribute aesthetic excellence to "this," any of these expressions will do. Even here I have incurred a criticism from Professor Muriel Bradbrook, who objected strongly that this was to give in most weakly to a sloppiness of expression. Someone who refuses to say "This is beautiful" when that is what he means is convicted of social ineptitude in the use of language. Let us, then, agree to the statement of the aesthetic judgment as "This is beautiful" and examine its implications. In this form it stands the best chance of surviving as the attribution of highest excellence in art.

Professor Austin's objection calls for more argument. He wishes to direct our attention to the ordinary everyday expressions and thinks that their examination will yield valuable philosophical results. This may be so, but I cannot help thinking that it is more suitable to concern oneself with the key concept rather than with the incidental ones. We have been trained as philosophers to admire Hume's apparent modesty, to prefer the role of a day laborer who clears the ground rather than the role of the architect who plans an imposing edifice on a questionable site. This opposition may be questioned. Why may the architect not plan his edifice on the site that has now been cleared? A day laborer works on instructions, and it seems to me that the time has come for us to look to the purpose of all this clearing of the ground. It begins to look rather like the modern shelving of responsibility. I propose, then, to concern myself unashamedly with the beautiful and the ugly rather than with the dainty and the dumpy. Philosophers are as sheeplike as ordinary mortals, and if someone writes an article entitled "The Dreariness of Aesthetics"[1] they begin

[1] J. A. Passmore, "The Dreariness of Aesthetics," in *Aesthetics and Language*, Oxford, 1954. P. 36.

to cast about to find out why aesthetics is dreary, never asking themselves whether it is so or not. They have not even noticed that the late R. G. Collingwood produced some of the most exciting work of the first part of the century in his *Principles of Art* and *Speculum Mentis,* to say nothing of the work of Edward Bullough and the fringe writings of people such as Gombrich, Empson, and Fry.

In their attempts to track down the source of the supposed dreariness, they dredge up the "mistake" on which traditional aesthetics is supposed to be based. This mistake is to think the main task of aesthetics to be the search for abstract and universal "beauty," which of course is not to be found. Now if anyone at all were to be tied to the search for universal beauty it surely would be Plato, but what do we find in his actual investigations?[2] We find him presenting Socrates as examining what it means to say of a horse, a maiden, a pruning knife, a porridge pot, or even of a dung basket that it is "beautiful," and the ensuing remarks might easily belong to a present day discussion. I am, then, simply thinking of the possibility that we might find any object pleasing in the required way, or not. If the required way is aesthetic, then the ensuing judgment would be "This is beautiful."

Corresponding to every judgment of value having as its subject the name of an object, event, state

[2] Xenophon, *Memorabilia,* trans. E. C. Marchant, London, 1923. Bk. III, Ch. 8, para. 4–7. Plato, *Hippias Major,* selections in *Philosophies of Beauty,* ed. E. F. Carritt, Oxford, 1931. P. 3.

of affairs, or even a statement, there will be a statement to the effect that "I approve" or "disapprove"
this object, event, or state of affairs. The nature of
the approval will depend on the nature of the object. If the object is an action or a human being
considered as an agent, the approval will be moral.
If the object is a statement considered as the conclusion of an argument, the approval will be logical.
If it is a statement of fact, the approval will be
harder to characterize—it might be moral approval
of a speaker of the truth or of a careful observer,
or it might be the simple common-sense satisfaction
of having a state of affairs rightly described. If the
object is a natural object or an artifact, the approval
will be aesthetic. A man may be judged as good
and his actions as right, a statement as true or well-
founded, and an object as beautiful. That is to say,
in place of "This S is P" we might put "I approve
this S." Here there are four possibilities: (1) I, this
particular person with all my idiosyncrasies, approve this object with all its peculiar properties.
(2) I, as a human being, approve this object with
all its peculiar properties. (3) I, this particular person with all my idiosyncrasies, approve this S and
all other objects like it in the appropriate respects.
(4) I, as a human being, approve this object and
everything like it in the appropriate respects. We
might sum up this system by opposing particularity
and universality and pointing out that these may
occur at either the subject or the object end.

P = as a particular person or object
U = as the universal person or object

I (P) approve O (P)
I (U) approve O (P)
I (P) approve O (U)
I (U) approve O (U)

(1) This would represent at least one aesthetic theory: to every man his taste. It could not apply to the approval of the truth of a statement or the rightness of an action. (2) This seems to me to be the legitimate aesthetic judgment. This particular object ought to be admired by everybody. It is incidentally true of rightness and goodness, but then we should be able to add that it is because "this" possesses such and such properties that everybody ought to find it good. However, it may be the case, and I think it is, that we shall not be able to add this proviso in the case of beauty. (3) This position appears to me not to be held by anybody about any object in terms of its value. It could be interpreted thus: "It is my personal idiosyncrasy to approve this and everything like it in the appropriate respects." (It is hard to see what "appropriate respects" could mean in this case.) (4) This seems the natural expression for the truth of statements, the validity of reasoned conclusions, the rightness or wrongness of acts, and the goodness or badness of agents.

We must first remove some ambiguities. First, I am not concerned with the judgment such as "This is a beautiful picture, poem, composition, play, and so on." In such a judgment, the object is evaluated as a specimen of a kind. It is a conceptual judgment with criteria for its truth, however hard it may be to determine the criteria. A purely aesthetic judgment is upon "this" as an individual. Even if there were relevant and universally acceptable aesthetic principles, they could be triumphantly broken by the next artist. Second, I am not concerned with the judgment such as "This is a beautiful pruning knife," in the sense that its qualities are both pleasing and such as to fit it for its purpose, though both these judgments contain aesthetic elements.

The third ambiguity is of a different order. Hegel, speaking of the sculpture of classical Greece said, "More beautiful art than this cannot exist, either now or hereafter." For Hegel, as we said above, self-knowledge of spirit had at that time reached a stage at which it could be sensuously presented with complete adequacy; that is to say, the conditions for beautiful art prevailed. The art of later ages had to struggle with a certain unmanageability in the material, and looking back at those golden days, one is tempted into the absurdity of speaking of "beautiful beauty." There is no doubt that for many people "beauty" has retained this connotation. They apply it to harmoniously proportioned statues and pictures, harmonious and rhythmical music and poetry, and refuse to apply it to discordant and harsh-sounding music and poetry, monstrous and disproportioned sculpture and painting. Thus, many modern artists disclaim beauty for their products and claim to be more interested in power, force, and strength. They cannot disclaim beauty in my sense; this would be to reject artistic excellence as desirable, which is absurd.

I am, then, concerned with the pure judgment

of beauty, however that judgment may be expressed. Since the object is not being judged as a specimen, nor as adapted to an end, nor as possessing certain specifiable qualities, but simply as eliciting the judgment of beauty, the judgment that it elicits will always be singular. It will also, I hope to show, be universally valid. In short, it is Kant's judgment of taste.

If A says of an object X that it is beautiful and B says that it is not beautiful, one of them is wrong and the other right. If the contradictory judgments were descriptive, there would be accepted ways of determining which of the two was right. Since the judgment invokes no concepts, we can apply no tests so far as the object is concerned. What we can do is to find out whether A and B are making genuine aesthetic judgments. It is interesting to notice that this is the procedure recommended by Hume in describing the expert in morals and art. Hume, the arch empiricist who professes to find no passage from fact to value, so that every dispute about taste can be resolved into a dispute about matters of fact, is, nevertheless, forced to recognize as a matter of fact a procedure to determine who is right about the attribution of beauty. This procedure does not at all depend upon observable qualities of the object. It is simply to find out who is the expert in matters of taste, though Hume ought not to allow any such person. Hume accepts expert opinion as a fact and describes the expert as one who is freed from the prejudices of his own time and country by wide acquaintance with the art of other times and places. He is free from per-

sonal preoccupations and interests and has been
trained to careful discrimination in his perception
of objects. In short, he is able to look or to listen
attentively, almost as if he were simply a human
being and not an upper-class Scotsman of the
eighteenth century. Such a man committing himself to the judgment of beauty upon an object, in
the same act claims the universal agreement of his
fellows. If he feels any doubt, as he may, for instance, when confronted with a new art form, he
will confine himself to a statement that as a matter of fact he found it exciting, amusing, delightful; he may even add that he thinks you will enjoy
it too; but he is not claiming your assent unless he
commits himself to the pure aesthetic judgment,
"This is beautiful."

Suppose we differ from the judgment of a man
so gifted, so trained, and in such a good position
for simply attending to the object. We first question ourselves very closely as to whether we have
private and personal grounds for our different opinion. We very often know that our judgments on
works of art are impure aesthetically. We know that
we cannot appreciate certain themes however
treated or that we tend to enjoy others too much.
However, if we can find nothing to prevent us from
seeing the object aesthetically and we still differ
from the expert, then it must be that one or the
other of us, though unaware of it, is incapable of
viewing the object disinterestedly. It cannot be that
we are both grasping the object simply as human
beings and that one alone pronounces it beautiful.
If *one* finds it eminently suited to human contem-

plation, if it calls into active play his understanding and imagination while maintaining its unity, then it must do the same to any other human being. To attribute beauty to such an object is not to attribute a quality, but to say that it is so constructed that it can be grasped as a unity in spite of its complexity and that it lends itself to growing acquaintance with it as an individual.

This seems to me to describe the way in which we occupy ourselves with works of art and literature. We learn more about them only in order to come back to them and apprehend them more completely. Delight in looking and listening so completely and understandingly is an authentic aesthetic experience, and this delight is one sign of the presence of beauty. Contradictory aesthetic judgments are not of the form A is B, A is not B; if they were, we could invoke reasons that the other person must accept. They are of the form "I, simply as a human being, pronounce this beautiful"; or "I, simply as a human being, pronounce this not beautiful." These are incompatible judgments, but since beauty is not a quality, it is not because one and the same thing cannot possess and not possess the same quality; it is because one and the same thing cannot present itself as beautiful and not beautiful to a human being simply as a human being. The contradiction lies in the claim of both speakers to speak for his fellows. One or the other is making a false claim: "I, finding an object beautiful, must call on you to find it beautiful too. Equally, you must call on me to agree with you under similar circumstances."

There are many other judgments upon works of art, many other valuable experiences in connection with works of art. It may even be that these other experiences are of greater human importance. There is no doubt that Hegel valued the works of Goethe and Shakespeare more highly as products of the human spirit than the sheerly beautiful sculpture of ancient Greece. It may even be that no work that is completely satisfying aesthetically can be great. Its very perfection may prevent the spectator from being powerfully moved. The Alhambra at Granada is a case in point. Everything is so perfectly matched to everything else and to the function of the building that it is simply beautiful, but not to be compared for one moment with, for instance, Chartres. However this may be, beauty has its own kind of importance; we may not be strongly moved by it, but for a moment stilled as though by a glimpse of eternity.

Having defended to the best of my ability my concern with the judgment of beauty and its objectivity, and having compared it in these respects with the judgments of morals and science, it now remains to compare them in a further respect. Our connecting of the judgment of beauty with moral and scientific judgments poses some questions that have tended to be oversimplified. For example, may we present as parallel pairs beautiful-ugly, good-bad, true-false? The question whether every action is right or wrong is relatively unimportant, that every statement is true or false is assumed, but that every object is beautiful or ugly is both doubtful and important. If we take the sphere of moral judgment as actions and the sphere of knowledge as statements, then what is the sphere of aesthetics? Is it "objects of perception" used very widely? The following diagrams illustrate my point:

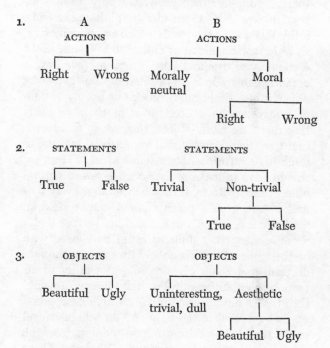

If we were considering whether the diagrams under A were more satisfactory than those under B, the answer would be different in the three cases. It is quite likely that there are many actions that are neither right nor wrong, although of course at this point we should be involved in a dispute as to whether in this case they were rightly called "actions." This is not our concern here. In considering group 2, most philosophers would say unhesitatingly that every statement must be true or false and that there is no higher dichotomy. The only possible exception would be those idealist philosophers who think that some statements are so fractionally true, so little worth making as almost to fall outside the dichotomy of true and false. In group 3 we have a genuine choice. It is a possible position that every object is beautiful or ugly though its beauty or ugliness may not be noticed. It is much more likely that there are many objects that are so uninteresting, trivial, and dull that it would be a mistake to think of them in aesthetic terms at all. (Here we should have to make a distinction between natural objects and artifacts. It may be true that every natural object, even a patch of mud, might yield an aesthetic experience, but it could not be true that a verse of staggering dullness could be viewed with aesthetic pleasure.) We should then choose the subdiagram and think of every object worthy of attention as either beautiful or ugly. Beautiful would then have a double opposition; it would be opposed on its own level to the ugly and on a higher level to the trivial. The third group also differs from the other two in presenting an unreal dichotomy. There are hundreds of intervening terms falling more or less to the right or left of the division. For example, "pretty," "charming," "elegant," "dainty," "garish," "fussy," "pretty-pretty" . . . "ugly." It might be said that the same thing is true of the right/wrong dichotomy, for example, the intervening terms "heroic," "cowardly," "mean." . . . Here, however, it seems that we are going outside the purely moral sphere. "Heroic" and "mean" seem to have a partly aesthetic flavor. Someone whose actions are "mean" is not necessarily wicked. We may notice a further distinction. While we must pass moral judgments on occasions, or at any rate we *do* pass moral judgments on occasions, it may be the case that we never pass aesthetic judgments on objects at all. I say it "may" be the case because this has been claimed by some aestheticians. My own opinion is that as far as explicit statement is concerned, it is just as likely that some people never make moral judgments as that they never make aesthetic judgments. Everybody certainly has to choose whether to do a certain thing or not, and a moral judgment may be implicit in our choice. Similarly, however, everybody has to choose between objects, between going one way rather than another, spending the evening in one way rather than another, and in these choices aesthetic principles may be implicit.

We may illustrate the singularity of the judgment of taste by a further contrast between the three types of value judgment. A man making a moral judgment calls on his fellows to agree with him that any action of that same kind must be approved or disapproved. A scientist surveying the evidence for a theory and finding it satisfactory calls on his fellows to agree that any conclusion so attested must be accepted. The same thing must be said of a piece of deductive reasoning. A man passing an aesthetic

judgment on a work of art calls on his fellows to
agree with him that this object, not this kind of object, is worthy of admiration. We may put it this
way: we expect everyone to agree that keeping
promises and speaking the truth are right, but not
that tragedies, for example, ought to be admired.
We think that *Hamlet* ought to be admired but
not tragedy in general. (Of course it may be that
for some reason peculiar to our own history we are
unable to admire *Hamlet*, but we at least know
that it ought to be admired.) I like to call such examples of compelling excellence "exemplary particulars." All of us can recall an outstanding occasion when we know for sure that we have had a
genuine aesthetic experience. It may be a particular rendering of a particular play or a particular
piece of music conducted by a particular man; in
each case, the "particular" stands for a model
against which we "place" other experiences as falling short or not. Such an experience stands almost
as the bronze yard measure kept in the offices of the
Board of Trade.

We may recall that in other ages there have been
notable cases of good or bad conduct taken to be
"exemplary particulars" for evermore. It is true that
these happenings are remembered as examples of
good or bad conduct, treachery, unnatural revenge,
or even cupidity. They are used as picturesque
moral reminders, while similar exemplary particulars in art remain as particulars. In *The Libation
Bearers* of Aeschylus the chorus waits outside the
palace while Orestes goes in to kill Clytemnestra

and Aegisthus.[3] They recall the dreadful deeds of
which women are capable but not in general terms.
"Learn truth from sad Althaea," they say, who
killed her son, and "Scylla, who sent her father to
die where swords were waiting." Finally, the Lem-
nian massacre,

> . . . *a tale*
> *To make men groan with heartsickness.*
> *And when they speak, all paled,*
> *Of some new outrage, "it is as bad," they say,*
> *"As what occurred in Lemnos."*

The men and women of the chorus are assuming
that any reasonable person, knowing of these terrible deeds, will perceive their awfulness. Similarly,
we all speak to one another of *Oedipus Rex, King
Lear, War and Peace,* the Brandenburg Concertos,
"The Virgin of the Rocks" and feel confident that
everyone will accept them as masterpieces. It is
true that our assumption is sometimes disappointed.
There are moral imbeciles just as there are intellectual imbeciles. There are people who cannot
follow a mathematical theorem and people who
cannot see that what is right for them is right for
other people too, and vice versa. Similarly, there
are "aesthetic imbeciles" who cannot "see" a mas-
terpiece.

Some people find this point of view very annoy-
ing. They feel confident that there is no disputing
about taste and that the most we can hope for is
an exchange of points of view. My point is that if

[3] *The Libation Bearers,* trans. Philip Vellacott, Harmondsworth, Middlesex, 1956. P. 125.

there are such disciplines as ethics and aesthetics, then we must assume that they are constituted a unity by some principle such as, "It is better to act rightly than wrongly, and to approve right rather than wrong action," "It is better to reason well and accept reasoned conclusions," or "It is better to admire worthy than unworthy objects." These are constitutive principles in that they do not form part of each of the three studies. We might compare them with the constitutive principle of medicine, "Health is better than disease." This is not a medical principle, but constitutes the unity of medical science. The doctor does not have to convince us that health is better than disease before he begins treatment. He assumes that that is why we have called him in.

At this point, it becomes important to notice the transference of emphasis from the aesthetic object to the experience. I want to maintain that an experience must be aesthetic not only in having certain characteristics, but also in being directed toward what I am calling "a worthy object." This is where I shall arouse the strongest antagonism. By what right, it will be asked, does anyone pronounce upon the worthiness of objects that give delight to other people? At this point, I can only appeal to experience. People put themselves to school to learn how to appreciate difficult works of art and see that their children have the opportunity of listening to good music and going to art galleries. We take the opinions of some people as more worth having than those of others because we feel that their opinions about the worth of objects are justified by experience, attentive perception, and thought. If this were not so, that is, if the objects they value were *not* more worthy of study than others, then their opinions would not be worth having. (Even Hume said that we all know that Milton is a better poet than Ogilby.[4])

What I have attempted to do is to rehabilitate the notion of beauty and restore it to respectable current use not only against the denigration of modern philosophers, but also against what we may call the trivialization of aesthetic inquiry. A concern for beauty is of the essence of our preoccupation with art, with our conviction of its importance, of our dismay and indignation at the destruction of our villages and city squares.

We have noted that beauty is one of those words that is ambiguous in a very fundamental sense. Most words are ambiguous, but some have a dangerous and not merely an allusive ambiguity. Examples of such words having an ambiguity similar to that of "beautiful" are "natural" and "simple." These words are given a connotation that arises from their connection with certain times, places, and social circumstances that are taken as giving the *true* naturalness, simplicity, and beauty. We have already noticed the connection of "true" beauty with

[4] Ogilby (1600–76) is a dim figure in English literature though he receives over five columns in *The Dictionary of National Biography*. Hume writes, in his essay "Of the Standard of Taste": "Whoever would assert an equality of genius and elegance between Ogilby and Milton, or Bunyan and Addison, would be thought to defend no less an extravagance than if he had maintained a molehill to be as high as Teneriffe, or a pond as extensive as the ocean."

a given time and place, and some examples will make the comparison with "true" naturalness and simplicity clear. Here is an extract from Jane Austen's *Emma:* MRS. ELTON: ". . . It is to be a morning scheme, you know, Knightley; quite a simple thing. I shall wear a large bonnet, and bring one of my little baskets hanging on my arm. Here,—probably this basket with pink riband. Nothing can be more simple, you see. And Jane will have such another. There is to be no form or parade—a sort of gipsy party. We are to walk about your gardens, and gather the strawberries ourselves, and sit under trees; and whatever else you may like to provide, it is to be all out of doors; a table spread in the shade, you know. Everything as natural and simple as possible. Is not that your idea?" MR. KNIGHTLEY: "Not quite. My idea of the simple and the natural will be to have the table spread in the dining-room. The nature and simplicity of gentlemen and ladies, with their servants and furniture, I think is best observed by meals within doors. When you are tired of eating strawberries in the garden, there shall be cold meat in the house."[5]

What is simple and natural is taken by the affected Mrs. Elton to be to go to a party on a donkey and to have the dinner spread on a table out-of-doors. Mr. Knightley rightly replies that what is simple and natural under *his* circumstances is to have dinner in the normal manner in the dining room. In *The Winter's Tale*, the party for Perdita and Florizel is naturally out-of-doors since there

[5] *Emma*, p. 319.

would not be enough room for all the guests inside a shepherd's house. This is taken to be the "true" simple and natural, and to copy its external marks when the internal conditions are lacking is to mistake the essence. What is simple and natural in one context is affected and complicated in another.

Similarly, in Mrs. Gaskell's *Wives and Daughters* the Duchess, who is to be shown off by a political charity ball, annoys her host by appearing, as they say, *à l'enfant* in a sprigged muslin with natural flowers in her hair and not a vestige of a jewel or a diamond. She would probably describe herself as "simply dressed," but for her to appear so dressed is as affected as it would be for a shepherdess to appear at a country feast in black velvet and diamonds. It is my contention that beauty suffers from exactly this kind of ambiguity. Instead of being understood in its context as that which is just right, just what it ought to be, its external marks in a particularly favorable period are taken as the essentials of beauty, which is consequently rejected as applicable to other times and places. The classical beauty of ancient Greece is taken as true beauty, and at other periods when harmony and rhythm are out of fashion this is taken to be a sign that the notion of beauty itself is out of date and needs to be replaced by some other notion.

When I said that what is beautiful is "just right" and "just what it ought to be," this was not in relation to the function of the beautiful object, but in relation to what it is, i.e., as something made by a human being *for* human beings. To define art in terms of being made by human beings for human

beings is to make an essential difference between
the beauty of art and the beauty of nature. It must
either be that art is as if we found it by chance scat-
tered about the world, or beautiful natural objects
must be looked on as if they had been made for our
delight. This would constitute no difficulty for a be-
liever in a beneficent Deity. From my point of
view, too, this constitutes no difficulty since I think
that art and nature are in completely different categories. If I had to choose I would rather say that
naturally beautiful objects are *as if* they had been
made, rather than that works of art were *as if* they
had come naturally into being. I am acquainted
with a family that lived in a house formerly owned
by Henry Moore. Every available outbuilding was
filled with pieces of rock and stone that Henry
Moore had gathered and brought home for their
exciting shapes. However, he had left them behind,
while leaving behind none of his own works;
though my friends felt guilty, they did, as a matter
of fact, carry out the pieces of rock and stone and
abandon them on the beach and in the country.
They certainly would have done no such thing with
works of art. I know of course that this is complicated by the fact that Henry Moore's sculptures
could be sold for large sums of money, but even if
this were not so, there would be quite a different
feeling in throwing away rocks eroded by nature
and rocks lovingly carved by human hands.

It is fundamental to my point of view that the
beauty of art is quite different from the beauty of
nature. This is not to say that art is more pleasing
and certainly not that I like it better, but for me

there is an element in the enjoyment of art that is absolutely lacking in the enjoyment of nature. This element is sheer gratitude and amazement that any human being should have been so full of insight, so gifted, and so willing to take trouble as to make this thing for our delight. If I am in an audience I feel as though the composer or the playwright is speaking equally to each one of us. It is not as if it were a political meeting and we were being roused to some common emotion; we each keep our own identity, but any one of us would be an equally good specimen for the receipt of what is being said to us.

CHAPTER VIII

The Scope of Aesthetics

In my early days of teaching, "Introduction" as used to describe elementary treatments of studies in books or in university courses seemed to me a much misused term. I began my teaching life in a very good American college, yet it seemed to me that all the "introductory courses" listed in the prospectus introduced the students to nothing. They were eager to learn and took introductory courses in mathematics, music, zoology, logic, in everything you can think of, and probably then went on to something quite different. This bothered me. Now, however, the matter presents itself to me differently. An introduction is essentially a presenting of a person or thing to give one the opportunity of following up the introduction or not. We introduce a person by indicating her and saying, "This is my sister." There she is to be presented, and you may decide that you would like to know her better. A study cannot be presented in quite this way; we cannot say, "This is aesthetics, there it is." We must present *something* as aesthetics, and what I have tried to present is a bird's-eye view showing the interconnections of the problems arising from such a study, the solutions which have been propounded, the new difficulties arising from the solutions, and so on. It is impossible simply to present problems and their possible solutions; it is essential that one engages one's readers in the activities described as "doing aesthetics." It is not as if you were being asked whether you liked a certain dish, i.e., whether you would like it prepared for you at intervals. You are being asked whether you would like to engage in certain activities, and the only way to find out is to begin. If you were beginning to skate, you would not straight away learn to do figure-eights, but what you would learn would later on be used in doing figure-eights. Similarly, I hope to have engaged you in actually working out the beginnings of the more fundamental questions that you may later pursue in greater depth. This is partly an apology for having raised many questions and merely suggested the lines along which a reply might be sought.

As well as giving the kind of survey outlined above, one also has a duty to present and give an account of what actually is going on at the present moment in the study under view. This is especially important when, as I believe to be the case now, what is going on is a kind of skirmish in the neighborhood, having as its object the uncovering of all kinds of concepts in the hope that some pattern will emerge that will throw light on our central inquiry. (I hope that this is the hope, otherwise what is going on is unguided and irresponsible.) We might compare these activities with those of archaeologists in Britain who are in hopeful attend-ance when builders descend on a site and begin to demolish whatever is there. They hope that something will be turned up that will test theories about Roman or Anglo-Saxon occupation of that site. We must remember, however, that they are probably under the direction of the master archaeologists who will fit their discoveries into a theoretical system, the outlines of which are already established. Without this, it would be as if star watchers all over the world were making observations in the hope that somewhere there was a Newton or an Einstein to whom the records would be useful. It might even be that they were hoping that the empiricist's dream would come true and that the recorded measurements would display an order such that it could not possibly be overlooked. Even a child would see that 2, 4, 8, 16 . . . is the beginning of a series. Much of the very good work that is now going on in aesthetics is in the analysis of the concepts used in critical discourse. This is "something going on in the neighborhood of the arts," and as such it is hoped that it will yield something of importance to aesthetics.

The concepts of aesthetics, or rather the concepts occurring in critical and aesthetic discourse, belong on many different levels. There are the grand general concepts of kinds of arts, poetry, painting, sculpture, musical composition, and so on; there are the concepts within these categories—the comic, the sublime, and the tragic; and then there are the concepts occurring at a lower level within critical discourse, such as the delicate, garish, and fragile, correlated with adjectives such as "sad," "gay," "lively," "appealing," and "repellent." At a still lower level, lower because we are now speaking of distinctions within the work, there are the concepts of form and content.

There are some ways in which we speak of works of art that we know are accidental. For example, a packer employed at an art gallery will say of a certain picture that it is "five feet by six" or of a piece of statuary that it is "fragile." He is using these descriptions in quite a different sense from the sense in which an art critic might use them. Size is not always aesthetically irrelevant, however; a critic might say that it was unsuitable to make porcelain shepherdesses eight feet tall or a miniature David and Goliath in marble. There is an appropriate size for works of art as there is for animals. It might be thought that I am confusing what pictures are *of*, with what they *are* in themselves. In some examples, as of the shepherdess, this cannot be helped because the objects represented have a bearing on their representation, but this need not be so. It is more suitable to have a large landscape in oils than in water colors. The delicacy of the medium has a bearing on the size of the finished work. (A very large painting in delicate colors would be likely to be insipid.)

Let us look at the notion of fragility. There is a real fragility that is connected with the brittleness of the material. We can say of a very thin glass vase that it is fragile because of the material, but if we are using the word "fragile" to characterize the *appearance* of the vase, there is no connection with the real property of brittleness. In the first case we

are warning anybody who has to handle the vase
to be careful. In the second case we are drawing
attention to a quality of the look of the vase. The
appearance of fragility is connected with such
properties as delicacy of coloring and of outline.
We cannot say that it is delicately colored and
therefore fragile, as we can say that it is made of
thin glass and is therefore fragile. We might, however, be able to say that it is delicately colored and
therefore presents the appearance of fragility, or
that it is deeply and heavily colored and so does
not present the appearance of fragility. But we are
always apt to be foiled by an artist who sets himself
to accept the challenge and produce a lightly colored object presenting the appearance of strength
and toughness.

The point of concepts used in aesthetic discourse
is to direct our attention to the important features
of the work. These features are important in the
sense that if they were not noticed, the work would
not be appreciated. Appreciation includes not only
correct evaluation, but also complete perception.
The mark of good critical work is evidenced when
we are led back to the work, appreciate it more,
and see it more completely. Concepts used in the
critic's discourse must be such as to set our attention in a certain way and so enable us to enjoy it
more completely. There is the danger, however,
that a critic may force his own perception of the
work on his hearers and so prevent them from coming with fresh eyes to the enjoyment of the work.
Producers and adaptors of the work of other people, part of whose function is critical, may err in

this way by underlining what they take to be important and so preventing the spectator from enjoying intentional ambiguities.

Some critics do not accept this account of their function. They think of themselves as producing a work in its own right, and not as existing for the purpose of directing attention to the work of somebody else. We may illustrate their point by a paradox. A literary critic is necessarily a writer. Suppose he writes so well that we are contented with his work and do not bother to read the work that was the origin of his inspiration. Has he then failed in his function? If my account is correct, he has failed in that he has imposed a new work between the original and its spectator-audience. He is a standing contradiction in the sense that he professed to direct our attention toward a work and has done it so well that we do not bother about the work in question. Walter Pater is such a critic. I do not know whether there are any critics of his stature at the present day, but I do know that there are many more people who read reviews of books than who read the books. Publishers tell us that there are many more books about books than books.

There is of course an ambiguity in the phrase, used of the critic, that he is "doing his work well." He is, of course, writing a book and "doing it well" might mean writing well and interestingly so that the reader is led on with pleasure to the end of the book; it might even be possible to read a cookbook in this way. As the writer of a book, Mrs. Beeton would have succeeded in this case, but Mrs. Beeton herself would wish to be judged as the writer of a cookbook, i.e., as somebody giving good, reliable recipes, and useful hints for the management of the kitchen. Ideally this is what critics should wish, that they should be judged for their ability to direct one's attention to valuable works and lead to their greater appreciation. A recent convention of critics agreed that their job was to present themselves as personalities rather than to present the works they were reviewing!

In speaking of the "accidental" qualities of a work of art we seem to be contradicting what was said earlier of its uniqueness and individuality. Here we must make a distinction. According to Aristotle,[1] Socrates as a human being necessarily has a nose, and as an individual accidentally is snub-nosed. In order to explain his having a nose, we may think of him as a specimen of the human race with the appropriate entrances by way of sound, sight, and sense from the world to his consciousness. To explain the snub-nosedness we should have to give a causal explanation, perhaps through heredity, through accident, or even in the case of some primitive communities through the deliberate shaping of a nose according to the common ideas of suitability. (Mingling of these causes occurs in the snub-nosedness of a bulldog, who is naturally snub-nosed and therefore useful in bull-baiting because it can hold on and still breathe and whose snub-nosedness is deliberately developed by breeders in conformity with the ideal of a bulldog.) Similarly in the case of a medicine—it may be es-

[1] *Metaphysics*, trans. Hugh Tredennick, London, 1937. Z5 1030B 30–31.

sentially temperature-reducing and accidentally in a bottle of a certain type. This, by the way, is out of date; I am assured that it is no longer "accidental" that a certain medicine should be in a certain kind of bottle. Poisonous substances in England must be in ribbed bottles. This really bears out my point. There is nothing in the nature of a poisonous substance that necessitates its being in a ribbed bottle; it is man who determines that it must be in a ribbed bottle so he will be able to distinguish a poisonous substance by feel—at night, for instance, when he is less alert. We cannot say "This is in a ribbed bottle, therefore it is poisonous" in the same sense in which we say "This contains arsenic and therefore is poisonous." The sense in which we connect two sets of properties of a work of art fits neither of these two cases.

In one sense, we cannot say of any of the features of a work of art that they belong to it accidentally. If it is cold and austere, then it is not accidental that it is prevailingly icy blue, and vice versa. (Here it is questionable whether "icy" belongs on the perceptual side or on the critical discourse side. There is a color in fashion cards called "ice-blue" but this might be a blend of the two kinds of adjectives.) It is only if a work of art is seen as of a *kind* that any of its features could be accidental. Sir Joshua Reynolds is supposed to have said that no successful painting could have a cold color at its center.[2] Thomas Gainsborough, resolved to prove

[2] *Discourses,* "The Eighth Discourse," ed. Roger Fry, London, 1905. Pp. 244–45. See also article on Thomas Gainsborough in *The Dictionary of National Biography.*

Sir Joshua wrong, painted his famous "Blue Boy" in direct refutation. If Sir Joshua had not been speaking generally, Gainsborough's painting would have proved nothing.

Although we cannot directly connect colors and moods, it seems as though we can say that a melancholy subject is unlikely to be presented in warm glowing colors or a delicate theme in brilliant scarlets and orange. If, then, philosophers of beauty succeed in producing a theory of beauty, they will have to show how it is related to the specific properties offered as reasons for valuing certain works of art highly. They will have to consider whether it is possible to produce an intermediate principle that says in effect, "This is the way in which specific works will be able to conform to the general principle." This would be a principle for each kind of art that shows how the general principle may be implemented in painting, poetry, music, etc. It may be that the general principle is such that this is impossible. If art is expression, and if moreover expression is complete in the mind of the artist, then Croce was right, and the differences between painting and poetry are trivial and connected accidentally with the nature of art. If one wished to disagree, one would have to examine the meaning of expression, what it was that was expressed, and why expressiveness is a ground for valuing a work.

This seems to be the crucial point. Where does value enter in? If we say that art is expression, then the question arises as to why expression is valuable. We can easily see that it might be beneficial to the person becoming able to express his feelings

and that somebody looking at the work and being
led to enter into its experience is also benefited;
but this is not to explain why expression and the
appreciation of expression leads to aesthetic value.
It is not even clear that this, as a matter of fact,
happens. If someone is appreciating a work and is
asked what it is he likes about it, he may give all
sorts of answers, some of which are irrelevant and
some of which do not even express what he means.
He stands before a picture, reads a novel or a
poem, or witnesses a play with full enjoyment, but
when he is asked why he thought it was good, he
may only be able to reply lamely and vaguely. He
might say, "Well, it was about a dog," or, "I could
just see why the man behaved in the way he did."
The reason we give for liking things, or even people, are very often not the things we value about
them at all. They are just some of the obvious qualities we happen to have picked on and that we are
only appearing to offer as a reason. We can make
the point clearer by contrasting it with the acceptance of a conclusion of an argument. People agree
that it is obvious that if X was the only person in a
room when something disappeared, then he was
the one who took it. If the only food that everybody ate was the meat pie, then that was the cause
of the food poisoning. In these cases people do not
hit on the accidental features, they know what is
relevant. In the case of moral judgment, it may happen either way. People sometimes hit on the wrong
reason for approving an action, but it is even more
likely that they will hit on the wrong reason, if this
has any meaning, for approving a work of art.

Aristotle offered some kind of explanation for the value of art as imitation. It is doubly valuable by being both pleasing and useful. It might be that it could not be useful if it were not pleasing, for people would not submit themselves to it unless it gave them pleasure. Everybody, says Aristotle, delights in imitation.[3] They like to recognize likenesses, and this recognition is a foundation of knowledge. This does not give us what we want, though, because delight in imitation is not a specifically aesthetic delight, and to exhibit the usefulness of art is to exhibit it as having instrumental and not intrinsic value. What we are in search of is some way of exhibiting art as valuable in itself and not for the sake of something else. It may be both, but its value in itself must be the specifically aesthetic. The value of exercise is said to be for the sake of health. It may be enjoyable in itself, but if we describe its nature we shall see that it is directed to the end of health. By calling the actions "exercise" we are detaching them from their context for a specifically useful end. To wave our arms holding Indian clubs is exercise, but to wave our arms holding a whitewash brush is to be redecorating the ceiling. Exercise, then, is detached from usefulness on the one side and attached to the value of health on the other. Whitewashing the ceiling may be a healthy exercise, but its end is to have a clean ceiling and its accidental result is healthfulness. To exercise with Indian clubs is accidentally enjoyable and essentially healthful.

[3] *Poetics,* trans. Ingram Bywater, Oxford, 1940. 1448 B5–14.

This kind of example is complicated by modern views about the connection between pleasure and health. Today the developing of the exercise movement would take into account both the easy pleasantness of the movement and the invigorating effect, but the end remains as health and not as pleasant movement. Now in the case of art we are left with nothing outside itself as the end. It may or may not be pleasant in the making; what shapes its development is not the end and not the doing, but something else. It would be a very queer kind of artist who was led to paint by the pleasantness of the movement of his arm with a paintbrush in it. But it is difficult to describe what he is doing in a way comparable either to the man who is exercising for the sake of health or to the man who is whitewashing the ceiling. Both the artist and the man whitewashing his ceiling will probably step back at intervals to look at what he has achieved. We know exactly what would yield satisfaction to the whitewasher—it would be a pure white ceiling, with no dirty marks showing through and the whitewash evenly distributed. There is no exact way of describing what will yield satisfaction to the artist—he might have been confronted with some specific difficulty and feel satisfaction that he had got over that, but a general satisfaction with the work as a whole cannot be described. That the satisfaction has been felt is enough if it has been felt by the artist *qua* artist. If Gainsborough, stepping back from his "Blue Boy," had said, "What about *that*, Sir Joshua?" this would not guarantee the value of his painting unless we interpolate an intermediate step, i.e., this is good and it runs counter to Reynolds' dictum. The important element is the goodness of the painting.

The goodness might refer to (1) the making of something valuable in itself; (2) the enjoying of an experience valuable in itself; or (3) the making of something that will lead spectators or the audience to enjoy an experience valuable in itself. The only answer, in short, is in terms of aesthetic value beyond which we cannot go. We assume the autonomy of aesthetics and all we can do is to see where the assumption will lead us.

We have now arrived at the conjunction of two tasks: to exhibit the place of the autonomous principle of aesthetics in the system of principles by which we make our choices and to show beginners in aesthetics where the study will take them if they pursue it further. What we have really come to is the necessity for an examination of the notion of importance. It is sometimes assumed that morality is overriding in importance; that is to say, that though there are separate and distinct systems of value, each with its autonomous principle, there might be circumstances in which the moral principle dictated one course of action, the aesthetic or the scientific, another. The question has arisen notably in recent years in science. The finding out of facts has in the past seemed so important that moral considerations took second place. At the present time, however, there have been notable examples of scientists giving up their study of certain problems because they were "appalled at the con-

sequences to human beings of their possible discoveries."

We must not confuse the two different statements that each of the systems of attributing value
has its own constitutive principle and each is therefore autonomous with the further statement that it
is not possible to compare each with the other in
terms of importance. A comparable state of affairs
is a set of sovereign states in the world, each autonomous but of varying degrees of importance within
the world community. Perhaps "importance" is not
quite the word to be used here; it is rather that
some of them constitute a danger to the peace and
well-being of the others. In the pursuit of the values of knowledge, of conduct, and of art, it may be
that the satisfying of one endangers the satisfying
of the other, and we have to determine how to
think about our course in such a case. There may
be a principle that stands over the set of constitutive principles, i.e., a principle that makes single
value systems into a higher system. If there were
such a principle, it would be that the nature of the
"material" for each autonomous discipline must be
respected. This would mean in the case of morals
that persons must be respected, and from this
would follow the particular laws for the dealing of
human beings with one another. In the case of
knowledge, it would be facts, and it would lead to
principles for the framing of experiments and reasoning upon matters of fact in such a way that the
facts were never distorted. In the case of aesthetics,
it would be the appropriate way of dealing with all
the materials that artists and craftsmen have to

handle, including not only media but also the sights and sounds yielding inspiration to the artist. To put it briefly, persons are the material for ethics; statements, arguments, and facts for logic; things, sights, and sounds for aesthetics; but the nature of the material in the three cases yields an over-all principle in a more important sense.

It is hard to imagine that any person would try to deny that persons are more important than anything in the world. Any given person, no matter how "unimportant," is more important than any thing, statement, piece of knowledge, or anything else that one can imagine. If this is true, then moral principles override any other. There are difficulties in this view. We know what people mean when they say that it would be ridiculous to allow a "small" moral consideration to outweigh a "great" aesthetic consideration. What they would have in mind would be some such situation as this: "May I tell a lie to prevent the destruction of a valuable painting?" Let us say a madman proposes to destroy all paintings in the belief that they are evidences of witchcraft. May I mislead him by saying there are no paintings in this gallery and so save our masterpieces? We should probably work our way around this difficulty by refusing to call a false statement made to a madman a lie, but there would be some people, Kant among others, who would take the extreme point of view of the ancient maxim "Let justice be done though the world perish."[4] I would commit myself to no more than the

[4] *Critique of Practical Reason,* trans. Thomas K. Abbott, London, 1937.

principle that we must not oppose "this unimportant person" to "this great work of art."

Perhaps a word should be said about importance and unimportance as applied to persons. Strictly speaking, this implies an impossible combination, somewhat like speaking literally of a "heavy angel." "Importance" refers to the place of a citizen in a community, not to the worth of a human being considered as a person. The worth of a person refers to the sense in which we are all equal in the sight of God. To weigh one person against another would be unforgivable if it were not impossible. It is possible only in terms of their function in a community. People like to please themselves with puzzles about who should be saved if we had to choose between a surgeon, a poet, and an ordinary man. My answer is that we ought to judge ourselves in terms of usefulness to the community and others by their intrinsic worth. Ordinary people ought to vote to save the surgeon but the surgeon himself ought not to agree. "Equality" does not mean of equal value to the community but simply of equal worth as persons. It is the sense in which people are equal in the sight of the law, or better still in the sight of God. This I take to be the foundation of the anarchist's creed—that human beings ought not to enter into relationships that will make it appear that some people are more important than others. Certainly, if we want a bridge built, then for the time architects, engineers, and quantity surveyors are the most important people. Therefore, say the anarchists, take care to disband a bridge-building committee as soon as the bridge is built and do not let the habit of estimating people according to their usefulness take possession.

I am hampered by never being able to decide whether ordinary people ought to be satisfied with being as good as they can, or as brave as they can, or whether it is required of the most ordinary of us to be saints or heroes. Is what is required of ordinary people to be moderately good, while the saint belongs to a different category? Is it even true that when he has done all he can the saint ought to say, "I am an unprofitable servant"? That is to say, no matter what we achieve, it is not as much as was to be expected of us. Similarly, is a hero an outstanding person, or is he ordinary and everybody else falling short of his stature? All that I am willing to commit myself to is that there is a hierarchy of values, the highest of which is concerned with the welfare of persons, and, granted that this is not involved, truth and beauty have equal claim. Perhaps I do not even want to oppose these two values. It may be that the values of art are also truth values, but truth about individuals and not universal truths.

I will now commit myself to a series of statements embodying what I take to be important in the leading of a satisfactory life considered from the point of view of aesthetics. These are controversial, and I hope that they will lead my readers to consider how far I am to be trusted as a guide. Before embarking on this I will list a few incidental questions that have intrigued me, but that I have not so far followed up, in the hope that some of you will follow them up and test your ability to apply the concepts which we have been considering.

First, what kind of an offense is forgery? I mean, of course, forgery of a work of art, such as that perpetrated by Hans van Meegeren. It is first of all a criminal offense. It is also a deception practiced against one's fellows, but is it in any sense of the word an "aesthetic outrage"? Van Meegeren's pictures, purporting to be by Jan Vermeer, gave aesthetic pleasure to many viewers. If one places a forgery, so far undetected, beside an acknowledged work and finds them both pleasing, how is the situation changed when we are told that the first picture is not by Vermeer? If aesthetic pleasure is in the appearance, nothing has been changed in the *appearance* when we have been given a fact about it. Our way of looking at it has been changed, but has it been changed in a legitimately aesthetic way? There is no doubt that there is a certain amount of professional snobbishness involved—we must admire the accepted things. My own feeling is that what has been perpetrated is an offense against knowledge, not exactly in the sense of scientific knowledge but of knowledge of an individual state of affairs. Suppose we think of "the works of Shakespeare" and someone produces what he says, with a fair amount of plausibility, is a hitherto unknown play. This new play would have to be fitted into its place in Shakespeare's development, would have to come between two of the established plays, and it might throw us off completely in our estimation of how he changed from someone who could write

Timon of Athens to someone who could write *The Tempest*. In short, it is the sin of falsification of history. In the spatiotemporal system of events there is simply not room for the interpolation of an imagined event.

Second, what is the difference between our reaction on the one hand to an emotional situation in real life and, on the other, to a work of art which arouses the same emotion? Henri Bergson wrote a treatise on the comic called *Laughter* (*Le Rire*). This appeals to us all as allowable, but suppose someone wrote a treatise on the tragic called *Tears*. This would not do at all, but what is the difference? It appears that we are saying there are two ways of reacting to a situation involving sadness, one by tears when it is real sadness and another by the dry-eyed contemplation of the imaginatively presented sad situation. The comic, on the other hand, seems to allow of laughter whether it is in real life or imaginatively presented. How is it that we are allowed to laugh with the comic characters on the stage, not merely at them, or is it that in real life we are also allowed to laugh at people as well as with them? Are there two kinds of laughter, one suited to a state of affairs depicted in art and the other to real happenings? Is there a comparable state of affairs in the tragic, in that we are allowed to contemplate a sad happening involving real people as if it were a spectacle? It may be seen that this is a question involving both aesthetics and the proper treatment of persons.

Third, how is emotion present in works of art—for example, where is the jealousy in a portrayal of

Othello? Let us say the real person is Laurence Olivier, who is not jealous, at least not in the way that Othello is jealous of Cassio on account of Desdemona. How can you say it is Othello who is jealous of Cassio when there is literally no such person as Othello? We in the audience are not experiencing jealousy, and the question remains, just where is the jealousy which Othello is "about"? It seems that we are being presented not with an analysis of the notion of jealousy we might get from a psychologist, but with an anatomy of a particular jealousy.

Fourth, in considering with Croce the notion of kinds of art, may not "Guernica" be said to resemble *Paradise Lost* more than it resembles "Déjeuner sur l'herbe"? And is not the latter rather like "Gather ye rosebuds"?

To revert to my credo, I said "a satisfactory life insofar as it is considered as embodying the value of aesthetics." This was to rule out the possibility that it might be said of someone living in poverty, in a slum, in captivity, or even in "single blessedness" that he could not possibly be leading a satisfactory life in a complete sense. This I do not dispute. I am simply in the position of inquiring—what, from the point of view of the life of the imagination, the background, mental and physical, of all one's doing, may be asked from the side of the makers of our houses, our cities, our myths and songs, of our entertainment in general, of all the pleasures of the imagination? Among these makers I place very importantly our own selves as guided by teachers, preachers, parents—in short, by anyone

who in any way can influence our ways of thinking
and our conduct.

I will begin with a reference to a Sunday supplement on gardening. There was an enchanting picture on the cover which might have been called
"Portrait of a Happy Man," (I think it was Fred
Streeter). He was in a greenhouse full of flowers,
looking out through the glass down which streamed
raindrops in a heavy shower. There he was, watching nature giving just what he wanted for his flowers; he was in shelter, enjoying the beauty that he
had largely created, while outside was going on the
natural watering of his less delicate creations. This
lies in the center of a range of intensely valuable
and pleasurable experiences from the mystical, in
which there is identification between enjoyer and
object, to the most detached and distanced enjoyment of a work of high art. In between, there are
the everyday ways, not exactly useful, not for the
sake of something else, ways in which we enjoy
ourselves such as walking through a lovely part of
the country. It is not just an enjoyment of ourselves,
nor is it just the enjoyment of the object. It is not a
merging of ourselves with the object as in mystical
experience. It is an enjoyment of ourselves as engaged with the object. Moreover, the object is complex and yields delight in the unfolding of its differences. This is in contrast with the pleasure of
lying in a hot bath, in which there is no complexity
to be observed. I have never been so lucky as to
have a mystical experience, but my nearest ap-
proach to ecstasy has been under one of the following set of circumstances. It has been either in

sitting in a warm greenhouse, the sun streaming in, possibly cold outside, and pricking out seedlings one after another, not thinking consciously, but somehow aware of what they will become. (It is noteworthy that the misplaced epithet "grateful" occurs in "grateful warmth" but not, as far as I know, with any other noun.) The other kind of occasion is picking scarlet runners, when one has to look up and sees the beautifully shaped and colored bean leaves and the scarlet flowers against either a blue sky or a gray, it does not matter which. The enjoyment is again the cooperating of one's own work with natural processes and the sheer enjoyment in the action.

This enjoyment of oneself in an activity is not to be confused with the enjoyment, say, of a dancer, who is not only enjoying his activity but concerned to present something to be looked at with pleasure. The only kind of exception would be the practical dance of primitive peoples directed toward the end of rain making or some other magical end. We might recall that when such primitive groups are asked to perform, even on a London stage, they have very often not gathered that they are to be looked at. They are "doing their thing" on a stage, and the critics are led to say something like "It was a delight to see the vivid enjoyment of the dancers, but they were so disposed that it was difficult to see what was actually going on."

There is not much we can do about the making of myths and fairy stories. All we can do is to see that those that have delighted generations of human beings should not be lost. We can also try to prevent the classics in art and literature from passing out of our acquaintance and trust to the changing of fashion to restore the making of works both to delight the imagination and to move us as powerfully as do the works of the present generation. We might usefully try to bring about the recognition of the importance of the arts in their own right, not as promoting or injuring public moral welfare. In this connection it is important to make people see that the enjoyment of art is in a very wide sense "life enhancing." If there were to remain a censorship, it might usefully be exercised from this point of view and make quite clear that there is a lowering of the tone of individual and public life that is not a moral lowering. In his *What Is Literature?*, Jean-Paul Sartre says, ". . . and if I am given this world with its injustices, it is not so that I may contemplate them coldly, but that I may animate them with my indignation, that I may disclose them and create them with their nature as injustices, that is, as abuses to be suppressed. Thus, the writer's universe will only reveal itself in all its depth to the examination, the admiration and indignation of the reader; and the generous love is a promise to maintain, and the admiration a promise to imitate; although literature is one thing and morality quite a different one, at the heart of the aesthetic imperative, we discern the moral imperative."[5]

This passage expresses for me not only the way art and literature should work on spectators and audience, but also the appropriate relationship be-

[5] *What Is Literature?* trans. Bernard Frechtman, London, 1950. P. 45.

tween an artist and his audience. The artist wishes to show us something he has felt strongly and perceived clearly, and we wish to "get it" as he meant us to. Sartre speaks of "generous love" and "admiration," and we naturally feel these emotions toward someone who has given up time and energy to the making of objects for our delight and enlightenment. It is the kind of emotion we feel toward someone who has thought about our needs and character and chooses or even makes a present for us that is exactly right. To say of a thing that it is a "present" is to ascribe no properties to it, only a place in a relationship. Just as a work of art might be a blueprint, a musical score, or whatever, so a present might be a set of rail and boat tickets, a scarf, a plant, etc. All that we can say of a present is that it was chosen by A to give to B on a given occasion O, with the intention of gratifying B. Similarly, a work of art is specified by its place in a similar system of relationships, with one difference however. A work of art has been made by A to give not to a particular person B, but to X, where X is any man, with the object of delighting and enlightening X. Although we must say "X" and not "B" in any given situation, it is *as if* we were each being addressed personally by the artist, not as this particular person, but as universal man. Gratitude seems to me the appropriate emotion toward our artists and a delighted recognition of their gifts when they choose so exactly the right word, the right color to speak as human beings to human beings. If we are ever disappointed with a present, it is because it shows plainly a lack of thought for the peculiar properties of the recipient and of the occasion. Here, specific properties of the object *do* come into account—we might be given a green scarf when we feel that anyone knowing us should know that we never wear green. Similarly, a work of art might possess properties that disqualified it from doing just the thing it had seemed the artist intended. The properties are to be estimated in the given context, and it seems as though corrections are made from this point of view. It is as if we were continually matching experience against expression to see if what we have said is right for the occasion of the utterance. This kind of perfection can be achieved only in "small" works of art—a song, a sonnet, a miniature. In a larger composition we look for an appropriate organization of parts, an organization that might display its own kind of rightness while the parts displayed the smaller perfection. Such a relation holds between the songs and the larger whole of a Shakespeare play as with "Fear no more the heat o' the sun" in *Cymbeline*. If one could take a larger view still, one might be able to see the "works" of Shakespeare as one whole, with the plays as parts with still smaller parts.

In 1769 Sir Joshua Reynolds delivered a series of discourses to the students of the Royal Academy as one of its founders and its first president. In his final discourse he speaks of Michelangelo, and this is his concluding paragraph: "I feel a self-congratulation in knowing myself capable of such sensations as he intended to excite. I reflect, not without vanity, that these Discourses bear testimony of my admiration of that truly divine man; and I should desire that the last words which I should pronounce in this Academy, and from this place, might be the name of—Michael Angelo." I feel a similar desire for the same kind of reason that my last reference should be to "that truly divine man," William Shakespeare.

Select Bibliography

The following is a list of some of the more important works in the history of aesthetics and the philosophy of art.

ARISTOTLE. *Poetics*, in *Aristotle's Poetics and Rhetoric, Demetrius on Style, Longinus on the Sublime*, trans. with introd. by T. A. Moxon (J. M. Dent & Sons, London; E. P. Dutton, New York, 1953. Everyman's Library, No. 901).

BELL, CLIVE. *Art* (Chatto & Windus, London, 1914; G. P. Putnam, New York, 1959).

—— *Since Cezanne* (Chatto & Windus, London, 1922).

BURKE, EDMUND. *A Philosophical Enquiry into the Origin of Our Ideas of the Sublime and the Beautiful*, Ed. with introd. and notes by J. T. Boulton (Routledge & Kegan Paul, London, 1958).

COLLINGWOOD, R. G. *Outlines of a Philosophy of Art* (Oxford University Press, London, 1925).

—— *Principles of Art* (Clarendon Press, Oxford, 1938).

CROCE, BENEDETTO. *Aesthetics*, trans. by Douglas Ainslie, 2nd ed. (Macmillan, London, 1922).

DUFRENNE, MIKEL. *Phénoménologie de l'experience esthétique* (Presses Universitaires de France, Paris, 1953).

FRY, ROGER. *Vision and Design* (Chatto & Windus, London, 1920; Meridian World Publishers, New York, 1956).

GOMBRICH, E. H. *Art and Illusion* (Phaidon Press, London, 1962).

—— *Meditations on a Hobby Horse* (Phaidon Press, London, 1963).

HEGEL, G. W. F. *Philosophy of Fine Art,* trans. with notes by F. P. B. Osmanton (G. Bell & Sons, London, 1920).

HUME, DAVID. "Of the Standard of Taste," in *Essays Moral, Political and Literary* (Oxford University Press, London, 1963).

KANT, IMMANUEL. *Critique of Judgement,* trans. with analytical indexes by James Creed Meredith (Clarendon Press, Oxford, 1952).

LONGINUS. *On the Sublime,* in *Aristotle's Poetics and Rhetoric, Demetrius on Style, Longinus on the Sublime,* trans. with introd. by T. A. Moxon (J. M. Dent & Sons, London; E. P. Dutton, New York, 1953. Everyman's Library, No. 901).

PLATO. *The Symposium, Hippias Major, The Phaedrus,* trans. by Benjamin Jowett, 4th ed. (Clarendon Press, Oxford, 1953).

—— *The Republic,* Books II, III and X, trans. F. M. Cornford (Clarendon Press, Oxford, 1941).

RICHARDS, I. A. *Principles of Literary Criticism* (Routledge & Kegan Paul, London, 1960, reissue; Harcourt, Brace, & World, New York, 1968).

SARTRE, JEAN-PAUL. *Literature and Existentialism,* trans. by Bernard Frechtman (Citadel Press, New York, 1966).

TOLSTOY, LEO. *What Is Art?* trans. by Aylmer Maude (Oxford University Press, London, 1930. World's Classics).

VINCI, LEONARDO DA. *Treatise on Painting,* trans. and

annotated by A. Philip McMahon, with an introd. by Ludwig H. Heydenreich (Princeton University Press, 1956).

—— *Paragone: A Comparison of the Arts,* introd. and trans. by Irma A. Richter (Oxford University Press, London, 1949).

WITTGENSTEIN, LUDWIG. *Lectures and Conversations on Aesthetics, Psychology, and Religious Belief,* Ed. by Cyril Barrett (Basil Blackwell, Oxford, 1966; University of California Press, Berkeley, 1967).

Listed below is a brief selection of recent books, articles, and collections of papers on aesthetics and art theory. It includes certain works of criticism that bear on problems in aesthetics.

BOOKS

BEARDSLEY, M. C. *Aesthetics* (Harcourt, Brace, & World, New York, 1958).

BROOKS, CLEANTH. *The Well Wrought Urn* (Dobson, London, 1960; Harcourt, Brace, & World, New York, 1956).

CASEY, JOHN. *The Language of Criticism* (Methuen, London, 1966; Barnes & Noble, New York, 1966).

CHARLTON, WILLIAM. *Aesthetics: An Introduction* (Hutchinson University Library, London, 1970).

ELIOT, T. S. *The Sacred Wood* (Methuen, London, 1934; Barnes & Noble, New York, 1950).

—— *On Poetry and Poets* (Faber and Faber, London, 1957; Farrar, Straus & Giroux, New York, 1957).

—— *The Use of Poetry and the Use of Criticism* (Barnes & Noble, New York, 1933; Faber and Faber, London, 1955).

EMPSON, WILLIAM. *Seven Types of Ambiguity* (Chatto & Windus, London, 1930; Meridian, New York, 1955).

GOODMAN, NELSON. *Languages of Art* (Bobbs-Merrill, Indianapolis, 1968; Oxford University Press, London, 1969).

HOSPERS, JOHN. *Meaning and Truth in the Arts* (University of North Carolina Press, Chapel Hill, 1946).

—— *Introductory Readings in Aesthetics* (Macmillan, New York, 1969).

LEAVIS, F. R. *The Common Pursuit* (Chatto & Windus, London, 1958; New York University Press, New York, 1964).

—— *The Great Tradition* (Chatto & Windus, London, 1955; New York University Press, New York, 1963).

LEAVIS, F. R., compiler. *Revaluation: A Selection from Scrutiny* (W. W. Norton, New York, 1963; Cambridge University Press, Cambridge, 1968).

LISTOWEL, EARL OF. *Critical History of Modern Aesthetics* (Allen & Unwin, London, 1933).

MARGOLIS, JOSEPH. *The Language of Art and Art Criticism* (Wayne State University Press, Detroit, 1965).

OSBORNE, HAROLD. *Aesthetics and Criticism* (Routledge & Kegan Paul, London, 1955).

—— *Aesthetics and Art Theory* (Longmans, Green, London, 1968; E. P. Dutton, New York, 1970).

READ, SIR HERBERT. *The Meaning of Art* (Pelican Books, Harmondsworth, Middlesex, 1950).

—— *Selected Writings*, foreword by Allen Tate (Faber and Faber, London, 1963; Horizon Press, New York, 1964).

VALÉRY, PAUL. *The Art of Poetry*, Vol. 7 of the *Collected Works*, Ed. by Jackson Mathews, trans. by Denise Folliot, with an introd. by T. S. Eliot (Routledge & Kegan Paul, London, 1957; Random House, New York, 1961).

WEITZ, MORRIS. *Philosophy of the Arts* (Harvard University Press, Cambridge, Mass., 1950).

WILSON, EDMUND. *Axel's Castle* (Scribner, New York, 1953; Collins, London, 1961).

—— *The Triple Thinkers* (Oxford University Press, New York, 1948; Lehmann, London, 1952).

WOLLHEIM, RICHARD. *Art and Its Objects: An Introduction to Aesthetics* (Harper & Row, New York, 1968).

COLLECTIONS OF ARTICLES ON AESTHETICS

BARRETT, CYRIL, Ed. *Collected Papers on Aesthetics* (Basil Blackwell, Oxford, 1965; Barnes & Noble, New York, 1966).

ELTON, WILLIAM, Ed. *Aesthetics and Language* (Basil Blackwell, Oxford, 1954).

HOOK, SIDNEY, Ed. *Art and Philosophy* (New York University Press, New York, 1966).

MARGOLIS, JOSEPH, Ed. *Philosophy Looks at the Arts*, (Scribner, New York, 1962).

OSBORNE, HAROLD. *Aesthetics in the Modern World* (Allen & Unwin, London, 1968).

PHILIPSON, MORRIS, Ed. *Aesthetics To-day* (World Publishing Co., Cleveland and New York, 1961).

SESONSKE, ALEXANDER, Ed. *What Is Art? Aesthetic Theory from Plato to Tolstoy* (Oxford University Press, New York, 1965).

WEITZ, MORRIS, Ed. *Problems in Aesthetics* (Macmillan, New York, 1959).

WIMSATT, WILLIAM KURTZ, Ed. *The Verbal Icon* (University of Kentucky Press, Lexington, 1954).

ARTICLES

(Some of the articles listed below are to be found in one or more of the collections mentioned in the previous section. The references given below are to the original source.)

BOUWSMA, O. K. "The Expression Theory of Art," in Max Black, Ed., *Philosophical Analysis* (Cornell University Press, Ithaca, 1950).

GALLIE, W. B. "Essentially Contested Concepts," *Proceedings of the Aristotelian Society*, Vol. LVI, 1955–56.

—— "Art as Essentially Contested Concept," *Philosophical Quarterly*, Vol. 6, 1956.

HAMPSHIRE, STUART. "Logic and Appreciation," *World Review*, 1952.

HOSPERS, JOHN. "The Concept of Artistic Expression," in Morris Weitz, Ed., *Problems in Aesthetics* (Macmillan, New York, 1959).

MACDONALD, MARGARET. "Some Distinctive Features of Arguments Used in Criticism of the Arts," *Proceedings of the Aristotelian Society*, Supplementary Vol. XXIII, 1949.

—— "Art and Imagination," *Proceedings of the Aristotelian Society*, Vol. LIII, 1952–53.

MARGOLIS, JOSEPH. "The Identity of a Work of Art," *Mind*, New Series, Vol. LXVIII, 1959.

SAW, RUTH LYDIA, and HAROLD OSBORNE. "Aesthetics as a Branch of Philosophy," *British Journal of Aesthetics*, Vol. 1, 1960.

SCHAPIRO, MEYER. "On Perfection, Coherence and Unity of Form and Content," in Sidney Hook, Ed., *Art and Philosophy* (New York University Press, New York, 1966).

SIBLEY, FRANK. "Aesthetic Concepts," *Philosophical Review*, Vol. LXVIII, 1959.

STEVENSON, C. L. "Interpretation and Evaluation in Aesthetics," in Max Black, Ed., *Philosophical Analysis* (Cornell University Press, Ithaca, 1950).

—— "On 'What Is a Poem?'," *Philosophical Review*, Vol. LXVI, 1957.

STEVENSON, C. L. "On the 'Analysis' of a Work of Art," *Philosophical Review*, Vol. LXVII, 1958.

WIMSATT, W. K., and M. C. BEARDSLEY. "The Intentional Fallacy," in W. K. Wimsatt, Ed., *The Verbal Icon* (University of Kentucky Press, Lexington, 1954; originally published in *The Sewanee Review*, Summer, 1946).

ZIFF, PAUL. "Art and the Object of Art," *Mind*, New Series, Vol. LX, 1951.

—— "The Task of Defining a Work of Art," *Philosophical Review*, Vol. LXII, 1953.

Index